Zucchini Bread

yl, Frank and Alice Indelicato's daughter, is studying to be a nurse
ikes to cook nutritious foods. Her brother Michael always has a bi
en and in this recipe she uses some of the abundant summer
ini.

oil
s sugar
gs, beaten
s grated fresh zucchini *or* 1 package frozen sliced zucchini
5 ounces), defrosted and run through food processor
s flour
easpoon baking powder
spoons baking soda
spoon salt
3 teaspoons cinnamon
coarsely chopped walnuts
spoons vanilla

d oil, sugar and eggs. Add zucchini. Sift dry ingredients together
add to zucchini mixture. Stir in nuts. Add vanilla and mix well.
into 2 lightly greased loaf pans or 1 Bundt pan. Bake 50 to 60
tes at 350°. Cool 10 minutes before removing from pans.

: Cheryl suggests that when zucchini is plentiful, you should freeze
2-cup portions. Then you can defrost it any time of the year to bake
asty bread.

Tomato Pick Up

r cold, as a drink or a soup, this simple beverage is a real friend on
cs, at football games, or on car trips. A *Meet Delicato* reader, Sarah
er, says she puts a smoked sausage in the thermos, fills it with the
quid, and when she's ready to eat, she has hot soup and a cooked
ge!

s tomato juice
ole cloves
lespoon lemon juice
2 teaspoons sugar
and pepper to taste
cup California dry white wine

bine all ingredients. Heat, but do not boil. Drink hot, or store in
gerator to drink cold or reheat later. Serves 6.

15 gallons Olive Oil - Star Brand
15 gallons Heinz Catsup
3 gallons Lemon Juice
15 gallons Red Wine Vinegar
salt and pepper to taste
3 - 4 pounds garlic that was put thru an osterizer

Marinate crab that has been cracked for nine hours.

handwritten annotations:
2 cups
2 cups tomato sauce
1/2 cup
2 cups
3 tbsp salt
1 tbsp pepper
5 tbsp garlic pour
cracked

Marinate cracked crab for nine hours

Onions In Wine

6-9-

A cool, refreshing relish to serve with ham. Also excellent with ham and

4 cups thinly sliced Bermuda
1 teaspoon salt
1/8 teaspoon white pepper
cups California dry white w
Parsley sprigs for garnish

ons, salt and pepper in wine and chill for several hours or
rnish with parsley sprigs. Makes 4 cups.

 variation: For a lighter, rosier look, substitute red onions and Delicato
of Cabernet and use plenty of freshly grated black pepper.

Portuguese Beans

We often serve these beans with steak, Italian sausage or barbecued
mackerel," says Dorothy. "And the best wine is a red—Zinfandel or
urgundy." Dorothy also says that fresh dried beans make a real
ifference.

pound pinto beans
cups water
tablespoons minced parsley
teaspoon pepper
dium onion, finely minced
teaspoon cumin
tomato sauce (8 ounces)
ices bacon
tablespoon salt
garlic powder

nse beans and place in water. Add parsley, pepper, onion, cumin and
mato sauce. Stir. Bring to a boil and simmer 2 to 3 hours, or until beans
e soft, but not mushy.

Cut bacon into 1/2-inch pieces and fry until crisp. Add bacon and
ppings to beans. Add salt to taste. Simmer for 30 minutes. Add more
mato sauce, if desired. Serves 6.

handwritten annotations:
1 tsp chili pepper
1 tbsp garlic powder
4 cups beans
4 cups H₂O
8 ~ parsley
4 tbsp pepper
1 tsp pepper
1 lg onion
1 tsp cumin
2 cans tomato sauce
ground beef
(optional 2 lbs)
1 tsp chili pepper
Hamb

Double the cups of H₂O to beans
: 4 cups beans + 10 cups H₂O

drop beans into rapidly
minutes. Remove from heat
sit for 1 hour. then drain out

Delicato Family Cookbook

Dorothy Indelicato

Wine Appreciation Guild

San Francisco

Delicato Family Cookbook
From the old country to the wine country, a history in recipes

A Wine Appreciation Guild book
All rights reserved
© 2015 by Delicato Family Vineyards

Managing Editor: Bryan Imelli
Special Editor: Corrine Cheung
Book Designer: K. Shinn, Jessica Lopez
Cover Designer: Diane Hume
Cover art by Lowell Herrero

ISBN: 978-1-935879-66-4

Wine Appreciation Guild
is an imprint of
Board and Bench Publishing
www.boardandbench.com

Table of Contents

Introductions

    The Gaspare Indelicato Story _____ 9

    A Time To Celebrate _____ 10

    Cooking With Wine _____ 12

About Wine

    Cooking With Wine. _____ 14

    Be A Matchmaker _____ 16

    Serving Wine _____ 20

    Barbecuing With Wine _____ 23

Appetizers _____ 27

Soups _____ 35

Salads _____ 45

Pasta _____ 55

Seafood _____ 63

Poultry _____ 73

Beef and Lamb _____ 89

Pork _____ 105

Vegetables _____ 115

Fruits _____ 125

Sweets _____ 131

Postscript _____ 141

Index _____ 142

Form 22
FEDERAL ALCOHOL CONTROL ADMINISTRATION
December 1934

Permit No. W - 663

PERMIT TO ENGAGE IN THE WINE INDUSTRY

To Indelicato and Sebastiano Luppino, d.b.a.
Sanjasper Winery,

4 miles North of Manteca, San Joaquin County, on
the west side of the North Manteca Road, ¼ mile
south of the French Camp Road.
Manteca, California.

Pursuant to application dated December 26, 1934 ...., you are hereby authorized and permitted, subject to compliance with all State and Federal laws, to engage in the Wine Industry, pursuant to the Code of Fair Competition for that industry, as heretofore or hereafter amended.

This permit is issued subject to the right of the Administration to limit the production and distribution of wine, to allocate the production thereof, and to provide for the orderly distribution of accumulated stocks in the manner provided in Article VII of the Code of Fair Competition for the Wine Industry, and subject to all other provisions of the said Code, as heretofore or hereafter amended. This permit shall not be taken or held to create any vested right as to any standard of profits or volume of business; or any right to engage in the manufacture or distribution of wine after the termination hereof.

This permit is conditioned on the observance by the permittee of the provisions of the Code of Fair Competition for the Wine Industry, as heretofore or hereafter amended (other than the provisions of Article III thereof), and such regulations as have been heretofore or are hereafter prescribed by the Federal Alcohol Control Administration applicable to members of the Wine Industry.

Unless sooner modified, superseded, suspended, revoked, or otherwise terminated, this permit shall remain in effect for the duration of the Code of Fair Competition for the Wine Industry.

This permit may, after due notice and opportunity for hearing, be suspended or revoked by the Director, with the approval of the Administration, for violation of any of the terms or conditions thereof.

This permit is not transferable.

Director Federal

Dated February 1, 1935

U. S. GOVERNMENT PR

OFFICE OF
SUPERVISOR OF PERMITS
DISTRICT No.

IN REPLY REFER TO 14-AT 2:4

TREASURY DEPARTMENT
Internal Revenue
BUREAU OF INDUSTRIAL ALCOHOL
ALCOHOL TAX UNIT
San Francisco, California

June 28, 1935

REGISTRY NUMBER: 4094

TO: Sanjasper Winery,
(Gaspare Indelicato and Sebastiano Luppino, copartners)
4 miles North of Manteca, on West side of North Manteca Road,
San Joaquin County, California.

Application having been duly presented and approved, yo
horized and permitted, subject to compliance with
laws or of the municipality in which any of t
ed are exercised,
4094 for the manufacture o

8

The Gaspare Indelicato Story

On March 3, 1911, 16-year-old Gaspare Indelicato set sail on the SS Virginia from the island of Sicily to New York. Accompanied by neighbors from his seaside village of Campobello di Mazara, he left behind his parents, siblings and a life of poverty and political strife.

While most of the Sicilians settled on the East Coast, Gaspare's dream was to come to California. With only a few dollars in his pocket, he first traveled west to the state of Washington to meet a friend and compatriot. Determined to become an American citizen, Gaspare filed a Declaration of Intention for Naturalization in 1915 and registered for the draft in 1917 while living in Pierce County, Washington. There he worked among the chimneys and kilns of Clay City, making bricks to support the industrial boom of the early 1900s. Clay City was hit hard by the depression so Gaspare decided it was time to move south to California.

Francisco and Francisca Indelicato, parents of Gaspare.

News of the Hetch Hetchy Water Project brought the prospect of a much needed job for Gaspare. After completion of the Hetch Hetchy Dam, Gaspare traveled to Lodi, California to work in the vineyards. There he met his wife-to-be, Caterina, her sister Serafina and Sebastiano Luppino, another young Sicilian immigrant. Gaspare and Sebastiano married the twin sisters and made the bold decision to purchase an old dairy farm in the agriculturally rich San Joaquin Valley. Together they leveled the property with two horses and a scraper, then planted grapes for shipment by rail to home winemakers in the Chicago area.

After Prohibition ended in 1933, business as usual was no longer profitable. After much discussion and debate, a decision was made: the only way to salvage their grape crop was to make wine. Once the necessary permits were obtained in 1935, (see opposite page) they purchased a few small vats from neighbors who no longer used them and made their very first vintage of 3,451 gallons of red wine which was sold to local farmers and friends.

In 1960, Gaspare and his three sons: Frank, Anthony and Vincent purchased the small enterprise then called Sam-Jasper Winery, from Sebastiano and his son, Antonio. After Gaspare and Caterina's deaths a few years later, the brothers decided to incorporate the business and Delicato Vineyards was born. Today, Delicato Family Vineyards is a successful, modern winery with national and international distribution. Still family-owned by the heirs of Gaspare and Caterina's three sons, the third generation of the Indelicato family proudly continues the winemaking tradition with the fourth generation still "in training."

Francisco Lagrutta. Caterina's father.

A special thank you to Dr. Gretchen Krueger of Wells Fargo & Company, San Francisco, who helped research the Indelicato family history, for which we are extremely grateful.

A Time To Celebrate

Wine has always been an intricate part of our family tradition. We consider wine a food, a necessary part of our daily meal and a part of our family social structure. Growing up, neither my husband or I was ever denied wine. Therefore there was no strong desire to overindulge. Wine is a food and that is how wine is to be consumed; nothing more, nothing less. Our parents were always there as role models showing us how to appreciate wine with food. We were taught how to enjoy wine and how to respect it for all its good qualities. We have in turn taught our children the same values.

Compiling the recipes and family history has been work, but fun also. I've learned how difficult it is to measure ingredients. All these years I've been using a handful of this and a pinch of that. That's how Mom did it. I didn't realize how difficult it is to put a "handful of this" down on paper. How easy it is when someone is standing next to you and can literally show you "how much" and how the end product should taste. Writing the instructions down on paper is an entirely different story. I would like to thank Arlene Mueller for her help in this effort. She taught me a great deal and I miss having her close by.

The gathering of the recipes in this cookbook has given me many rewards. I've rekindled old friendships and have made some new ones. Some recipes that may have been lost will now be saved for future generations. I experimented with the old recipes and improved upon some of them. By publishing this cookbook, I've piqued the interest in cooking the old recipes by the younger relatives. I feel confident our family traditions will at least survive another generation.

I've also noticed the rippling effect this project has had on the friends and relatives I've asked to critique our recipes. They are beginning to recognize how important tradition is to them as a family. This caused them to investigate their own family food treasures.

It is my plan to continue collecting family recipes. I've become so much more aware of the foods family members prepare that I have long taken for granted. I've taken to observing and writing those observations down before all is lost (see the inside of the book cover for proof of this).

Papa, circa 1912.

Collecting stories for the history portion of the book allowed my mind to search back: I can remember as a youngster my mother telling me, when she was only nine years old, how she literally stomped grapes for her father. He was a Portuguese immigrant newly in the United States from Sao Miguel Island, Azores. He didn't have any of the equipment that is available today. She learned the old country ways of making wine with her feet. Part of my grandfather's wine cellar is in our home wine cellar today. My grandmother gave me Grandpa's old spigot that he used in the 1920 era to remove the wine from the barrels. I can remember how my grandmother, as she got along in years, always had a glass of Port before retiring in the evening. Her doctor had recommended this "remedy" in lieu of pills. She claimed the doctor said she needed to improve the quality of her blood and that she needed to relax before going to bed. We saw to it that Grandma always had plenty of "medication."

As the collection of family history grew, many new stories came to light. This one especially touches my heart. My father-in-law, in his younger days, delivered 50 gallons of wine to his customers. That means each day he loaded 400 pounds onto the delivery truck: the wine weighed 300 pounds and the wood barrel another 100 pounds! In his zeal to feed his growing family, he delivered barrels of wine day after day, putting this difficult strain on his body. He was a stocky, muscular man but this heavy burden took its toll. I can remember how carefully he walked -- silently enduring the back pain that was a result of his need to feed and clothe his family. I remember him as a kind, gentle man that my children loved dearly and there are many happy memories that we love to share with others about him.

I would like to thank my husband, Vince, for reminding me of several special memories and stories from our family's history. Some would have been forgotten had he not jogged my memory. I would also like to thank my daughter, Marie Indelicato Mathews, who helped to clarify and edit some of these stories.

In the process of constructing this book, picture by picture, recipe by recipe, my life has been enriched many times over. I hope that, in some small way, your family's traditions can also be enriched by reading our stories and sampling some of our favorite dishes. I know that family, food and wine is one way to experience the good life.

— Dorothy Indelicato

Dorothy Cardoza Indelicato spent her childhood within sight of the vineyards. In 1954, she married Vincent Indelicato, current board chairman of Delicato Family Vineyards. Today, in addition to the duties as Treasurer of the winery, she performs community service and charity work. At home, she prepares dishes from her husband's Italian heritage as well as recipes from her own family's Portuguese background. Her interest in preserving the Indelicato traditions and winemaking history is evident throughout this book.

Cooking With Wine

This cookbook puts the good life within your reach. It shows how to prepare delicious, wholesome foods at moderate cost without spending all day in the kitchen. The recipes that follow feature nutritious ingredients, convenient preparation, and the good taste that comes from cooking with wine.

Good health is essential to the good life. Vegetables and fruits account for over 96 recipes. The book offers more than 25 distinctly different poultry recipes plus plenty of good fish dishes. Frying and sautéing are kept to a minimum.

I advise "salt and pepper to taste," but have tested the recipes using little or no salt. Because wine adds natural flavor to a dish, you'll find that salt usually can be reduced or omitted.

Fresh ingredients are crucial. Buy what's in season for maximum flavor. Bring home the most succulent fruits, perkiest vegetables, freshest fish and meat from the market, then select a recipe from this book, put on your apron and begin cooking.

Convenience is a key consideration. You will save time and money because you can pick up the ingredients in a single stop at the supermarket. The phrase "available at specialty shops" does not appear in these pages.

Wine is a flavor component of many recipes, from everyday meals to dishes for company. Wine is essential for good taste in these recipes, not just something added to boost ordinary fare into the "gourmet" realm.

As you cook your way through the book, wine will begin taking its place in your kitchen alongside favorite herbs and spices. Soon, you'll find yourself adding a dash, a tablespoon, or a cup of wine to other recipes as you create your own unique dishes.

Castle Elementary School: Vince in first grade, Tony in fifth grade, 1939.

About Wine

Cooking with Wine

Mama and Papa's wedding picture, 1921

Q: What wine should I use for cooking?
A. Most wines can be used for cooking, but if you're new to cooking with wine, start with three basic wines: Chardonnay, Zinfandel, and a dry or medium-dry California sherry.

Q: Will recipes taste better if I use a premium or expensive wine?
A: A good wine will give the same fine flavor to a dish as a premium wine, so save the premium wine to serve with the meal.

Q: What is "cooking sherry"?
A: "Cooking sherry" usually has salt or chemicals added to make it unpalatable as a sipping wine (and to keep the kitchen help sober). Sold in small bottles, it is generally more expensive than regular sherry. When "cooking sherry" is called for in a recipe I recommend using regular sherry.

Q: Will I gain weight if I cook with wine?
A: Not from the wine. The calories from a dry dinner wine are insignificant compared to any other ingredient plus much of the alcohol may be burned off during the cooking process.

Q: Does marinating with wine make a difference?
A: Yes. A wine marinade accents flavors and helps tenderize meat. It is particularly good for accentuating individual fruit flavors and maintaining natural fruit colors. A marinade can often be strained and reserved as an addition to the cooking pot or final sauce.

Q: At what point in the recipe should I add wine?
A: It depends on what taste you are trying to achieve.
- For a **mellow** flavor, add wine at the start of the cooking process.
- To achieve a more **pronounced** wine flavor, reduce the wine by heating it in an uncovered pan. (One cup of wine will reduce to 1/2 cup in 5 minutes.) Stir the reduced wine into the food at the end of cooking process.
- To give an **intense** flavor to soups, gravies or sauces, add wine as you remove the food from the heat, when the cooking process is complete.

Q: Can I use leftover wine for cooking?
A. Yes. To save leftover wine for cooking, pour into smaller bottles, cork tightly and store in the refrigerator. However, never use oxidized wine. Only use wines in cooking that you would enjoy drinking.

Q: What are some suggestions to make a dinner extra special?
- Serve a small glass of sherry alongside soups and invite your guests to stir in as much sherry as they wish.
- Stir wine into pan drippings for a quick sauce or gravy.
- Wine should be added before milk, cream, eggs or butter to avoid curdling or separation.
- Add heated wine (hot, but not boiling) to meat dishes as a tenderizer.
- Brown the meat before adding wine.

Q: Should all cooking wines be kept in the refrigerator after they are opened?

A: Yes, with the exception of sherry and port. Because of their higher alcohol content (about 20 percent), a partly filled bottle will keep a couple of months in the cupboard after opening. However, if your kitchen gets hot (in the summer, for example), store the sherry in the refrigerator.

To keep wine on hand just for cooking, float a thin film of cooking oil on the surface to seal the wine from air oxidation.

Q: Can I add wine to any recipe?

A: Some wine enthusiasts maintain that all foods improve with the addition of wine. Experiment with a familiar recipe to see how wine changes flavors then decide how much and when to incorporate wine into your recipes.

Q: How much wine should I add?

A: That depends upon the flavor intensity of the wine and the foods you are cooking. Proceed slowly in trying new combinations. Wine needs time to impart its flavor. If you're not sure whether to add more wine, let the dish cook at least ten minutes before tasting again.

Q. When following a recipe how can I estimate the amount of wine to add?

A: When following a recipe, include wine in the total liquid ingredients, not as an extra amount. If you add wine, deduct a like amount of other liquid from the recipe. Sherry has a more intense flavor than red or white wine, so it should be used in smaller amounts. For example, 2 tablespoons of sherry has the same flavor intensity as 1/2 cup of red or white wine.

Suggested Amounts:

Soups—2 tablespoons per cup	Stews and Meats—1/4 cup per pound
Sauces—1 tablespoon per cup	Poaching (fish)—1/2 cup per quart
Gravies—2 tablespoons per cup	

THE EARLY YEARS

People came to the house all the time to visit with Dad. The house would be filled with the Italian language, for most of the folks' friends were immigrants, too. Although Dad learned English, Mom never did.

Mom boiled strong coffee, strained it, then added lots of cream and sugar—and Dad got out a jug of his red wine.

After pouring everyone a small tumbler, just like the ones our relatives still use in Sicily, he set the jug on the floor by his chair. He was in charge of the wine and never failed to notice when a glass needed refilling.

Dad loved food and wine. "Let's eat," he'd say with a hearty laugh, "for that's all we have in this world."

As the visitors sat around the big table laughing and talking, Dad would lean back and light up a black Toscannelli cigar.

When the guests prepared to leave, he filled boxes with vegetables and fruits from his garden for them to take home. "This doesn't cost anything," he'd say. "We've never been short of food."

— Tony Indelicato

Be A Matchmaker

Consider two things when "marrying" wine to food. First, match your food with a wine that complements it so there will be no struggle between the two. The old adage, "opposites attract," does not apply here. You don't want a robust Petite Sirah saying to the delicately flavored pork roast, "I'm the strongest!" Instead, the pork roast should join with a milder red, such as a fruity Zinfandel, so they can sing together: "We make a great pair."

Second, match the wine with the food so that neither loses its unique flavor. Cabernet Sauvignon, a full-bodied red wine, is smooth, with no discernable acidity when served alone or with tart foods. But pair the Cabernet to a ham glazed with candied fruit sauce and the same wine will taste unpleasantly acidic because of the contrast. Like a good marriage, the pairing is most successful when both members retain their own characteristics, yet contribute to the total combination.

FLAVOR FORMULA:
FOOD FLAVOR INTENSITY + WINE FLAVOR INTENSITY = BALANCE.

Choosing the right wine for the right meal is more than following the simple rule, "Red wine with red meat, white wine with white meat, and rosé wines with either."

The secret of successful matchmaking is to pair these three flavor intensities:

Delicate   Moderate   Abundant

First identify the food flavor intensity. Venison, mackerel, salami, garlic, broccoli and papaya, for example, have Abundant flavor intensities. No sauce or accompanying dish can tone down these assertive flavors. These foods call for an Abundant wine.

The flavor intensity of some foods is determined by the spices, herbs, sauces, and method of preparation. Beef, for example, has a distinct flavor but can be classified Moderate or Abundant, depending on how it is prepared. If the beef is grilled with a simple wine sauce, it would be a Moderate-flavor food. However, if the sauce included Worcestershire, capers, or horseradish, the flavor would become Abundant and call for a bigger, bolder wine.

Gaspare and his friends traveled through Ellis Island, New York in 1912.

Visualize three simple pizza crusts: top one with Mozzarella cheese and fresh mushrooms. On the second crust, place the same amount of cheese and mushrooms but add onions and green peppers. The third crust gets all the ingredients plus anchovies and pepperoni. Each pizza represents a flavor intensity level and requires a different wine.

To match wine and food intensities, you might try these combinations::

Delicate pizza: Mozzarella cheese and mushrooms = Pinot Grigio

Moderate pizza: Add onions and green peppers = Zinfandel

Abundant pizza: Add anchovies and pepperoni = Cabernet Sauvignon

After you've identified the flavor intensity, match a wine with your recipe, following the Flavor Formula

FOOD FLAVOR INTENSITY + WINE FLAVOR INTENSITY = BALANCE

The food and wine flavors will complement each other while maintaining the unique characteristics of both.

Here is a list of common California wines identified by flavor intensity:

Papa, second from right, with newly found friends he met in Washington State.

FLAVOR INTENSITY OF POPULAR CALIFORNIA WINES

DELICATE	MODERATE	ABUNDANT
White Wines Sparkling Wine Riesling Pinot Grigio Moscato White Wine Blend	**White Wines** Chardonnay Sauvignon Blanc Rhine	**White Wines** Chardonnay Sauvignon Blanc
Red Wines Red Wine Blend	**Red Wines** Zinfandel Pinot Noir Merlot	**Red Wines** Zinfandel Petite Sirah Syrah Malbec Cabernet Sauvignon

Some wines, like Zinfandel, appear in more than one category because winemaking styles, micro-climates and blending practices differ. A Zinfandel from one winery may be light and fruity (Moderate), while a Zinfandel from another winery is hearty and assertive (Abundant). As you become acquainted with individual wine varieties and winemaking styles, you will be able to predict the flavor intensity of a particular wine.

A Perfectly Matched Chicken

A perfect match takes into account not only the meat, fish or poultry, but also the accompanying dishes, the herbs, spices, sauces and the method of preparation.

Chicken is traditionally paired with white wine. Yet, when using the Flavor Formula (e.g. Delicate + Delicate = Balance), you could come up with all these tasty combinations:

Delicate-flavor Food with Delicate-flavor Wine

Chicken With Okra (page 81).Sautéed chicken pieces are touched lightly with garlic and onion then combined with the fresh green flavor of okra. Serve with rice and steamed carrots.
Wine Suggestion: Pinot Grigio.
> or

Chicken In Moscato (page 78). Creamy chicken pieces are surrounded by the sweetness of onions and raisins. Serve with brown rice and chopped spinach dusted with nutmeg.
Wine Suggestion: Moscato.

SAM JASPER WINERY
Bonded Winery No. 4094
Rt. 1, Box 304 – Telephone 39-F-12
MANTECA, CALIF.

License No. _____ Date 6-2 19 53

To San Francisco Supermarket

Address San Francisco 130 6th St

15 ca 1/5, 10-sherry, 5-Musc	61	50
2 ca 1/5 Port	8	20
4 ca 1/5 gal, 2-Tokay, 2-Musc	21	00
2 ca 1/5, 1-Burg, 1-claret	7	00
1 ca 1/2 gal Burg	3	55
1 ca gal Burg	4	00
	105	20
4% discount	4	20
	101	00
empties 25	3	25
	97	75

MADE FOR ZELLERBACH PAPER CO. STOCKTON BY SUNSET-McKEE SALESBOOK CO.

Invoice written out by Gaspare in 1953.

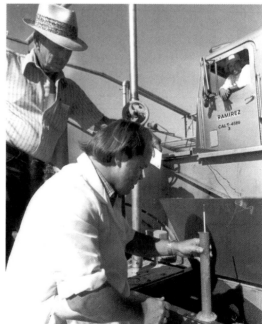

Chemist Glenn Lewis measuring sugar content of the must, under the supervision of Crush Foreman Joe Cardoza, father of the author.

Harvest 1980.

Moderate-flavor Food with Moderate-flavor Wine:

Chicken With Nutmeg (page 79). Onion sweetness combined with cilantro, nutmeg and sherry demand this chicken match up with a smooth and slightly assertive red wine.
Wine Suggestion: California Zinfandel.

or

Roast Chicken With Sesame Sauce (page 77). Serve this crisp bird with a potato soufflé and spinach-bacon salad.
Wine Suggestion: **Sauvignon Blanc.**

Abundant-flavor Food with Abundant-flavor Wine:

Chicken On The Hot Side (page 85). Although simmered and baked in white wine, this chicken lights up with pepper and Tabasco sauce. Serve over fettuccine with crisp salad greens.
Wine Suggestion: Zinfandel or Cabernet Sauvignon.

or

Mustard Chicken (page 76). Prepared with Sauvignon Blanc, country-style Dijon mustard and sour cream. Serve with mounds of white rice, sautéed carrots and zucchini.
Wine Suggestion: Petite Sirah.

Vincent, Caterina, Frances, Frank, Gaspare, Anthony, circa 1939.

In 1975 Vincent visited
his aunt in Sicily

Make friends with your Taste Memory

Taste memory, your personal ability to remember the taste of a particular dish, plays an important role in choosing a wine. Each of us craves comfort foods on our birthdays, holidays or milestone occasions. Think of your special foods and close your eyes. Imagine the taste and focus on the dominant flavor. Is it salty, sweet, nutty, spicy? When you've identified the dominant taste, memorize it.

Next reach for an imaginary glass of wine to accompany this taste. Practice memorizing the tastes of wine and foods at meals. Keep notes and suggestions for food and wine pairings in your recipe file, in the margins of your cookbooks or in a notebook just for this purpose.

Eventually you'll be able to read a recipe and "taste" a wine to match it. Soon food and wine will go together easily and you'll avoid those frantic, last minute wine purchases. You may want to start your own wine cellar so your favorite wines will always be on hand.

A Final Word

There are no firm and fast rules for matching wine and food, only guidelines and suggestions. Your personal taste in both food and drink must determine your final choice.

Serving Wine

Today, most entertaining is dictated not by etiquette books but by individual tastes. The way you serve wine should reflect your own style of hospitality. Here are some simple suggestions that will make your wine service more attractive while preserving a touch of tradition.

Which Wines?

First decide on a menu, then choose the wine. If you have your own cellar, get the wines out in the morning and place them upright. If you are purchasing wines, buy them the day before serving, since wines don't like movement or temperature changes before they're opened.

How Much Wine?

The standard wine bottle is 750 ml, one "fifth" of a gallon, or 25 ounces. This will provide four servings, using a nine-ounce all-purpose glass.

Champagne portions are generally smaller, so expect to serve six guests from each 750 ml bottle.

For a dinner preceded by drinks or aperitifs, plan on one-fourth bottle per guest. If dinner is to be leisurely, with several courses, allow one-half bottle per person. If you are serving several wines, determine quantity in the same way, allowing one-fourth bottle per guest for each course. Amounts vary, of course, according to the length of the dinner and the desire of the diner.

What Temperature?

The "room temperature" often recommended for red dinner wines is actually closer to cellar temperature (65°F). If your reds are coming from a cooler storage area, bring them out a few hours before serving and let them warm up to 65°F. If your reds are too warm, chill them briefly in the refrigerator. Watch the temperature, however: chilling red wines below 65°F brings out the tannin and results in a harsher taste.

White dinner wines should be chilled to 55° F and brought directly from the refrigerator to the table or to an ice bucket. Whites lose their bouquet, and consequently their best taste, if they get too cold.

Rosé wines are best served slightly more chilled at 45°F. Sparkling wines must be served cold, cold, cold: 35° F.

Ideal Serving Temperatures
Red Wine 65°F
White Wine 55°F
Rosé Wine 45°F
Sparkling Wine 35-45°F

These temperatures are ideals. You can check the temperature in your refrigerator with an outdoor thermometer. Place it on top, middle and bottom shelves to see which area is best.

How To Chill?

Champagnes and white wines can be quickly chilled in an ice bucket filled equally with ice and water. Total immersion and rotation insure quick chilling.

As a last resort for a fast chill, put the bottles in the freezer compartment of your refrigerator for 30 minutes. Set your timer so you don't forget them!

What Order To Serve Wines?

If you are serving several wines with your meal, you may want to follow the traditional rule: white before red, young before old, light before robust, and dry before sweet.

In this fashion you advance from delicately flavored foods and wines to more complex, abundantly flavored ones. The dessert wines -- sweet sherries, ports, late harvest, or fruit wines -- are sweeter and heavier and go well at the meal's conclusion.

Wines on a Picnic

Here's how to keep wine chilled on a picnic:

1) Chill the wine bottle in your freezer for 20 minutes before leaving home, then place it in your cooler with ice.
2) Soak several pages of newspaper in water until limp. Wrap the bottle securely and place it in your freezer until the paper is "crisp." Wrap in a towel and place in your picnic basket. The wine will stay chilled for hours.
3) Place chilled wine bottles in insulated containers especially designed for wine travel.
4) Or, go natural—tie a rope around your bottle and let it bob in the cold stream or lake.

To Serve...
If your picnic is an elegant affair, wrap wine glasses in napkins. If you're going casual, use clear plastic stemless glasses or small jelly jars. Pour small portions and offer refills to keep the wine chilled.

Kind of Wine

What Kind of Wine?
Although you should drink what you like any time of year, most people prefer light-bodied wines during the summer months. Try these favorite Delicato picnic wines: Viognier (with fruits and seafood salads), Chardonnay (with chicken dishes), Pinot Grigio (with cheeses and fruits), and Zinfandel (with barbecued meats). Delicato white wines make excellent warm-weather cocktails. Just pour wine over ice and add a twist of lemon. Like red wines? You can turn any red into a wine cooler by adding ice and soda water.

Glassware

Red

White

Champagne Flute

Champagne Saucer

Port

Grappa

What Kind Of Glasses And Where Do They Go?

An all-purpose, nine-ounce glass will do nicely for all types of wine, including dessert and sparkling wines. The tulip shape, narrower at the bottom and top, captures the wine's appealing aroma (sense of smell accounts for ninety percent of our taste sensation).

If you want to expand your glassware collection, add tall champagne flutes. This shape of glass keeps the wine bubbling happily.

Another useful glass to have is the balloon bowl glass, also called the big Burgundy glass. This large, open bowl gives ample room for robust reds to stretch comfortably. (Don't get carried away by the size when you pour: fill only one-third full, leaving space to swirl the wine and encourage the aroma.)

The hock or Rhine glass, a small bowl atop a long stem, is traditional for Rieslings and Gewürztraminers.

Clear glass is best since it reveals the natural color of the wine. Stemmed glasses keep hands from warming the wine and the bowl clear of finger prints.

If you have separate wine glasses for each wine, line them up to the right of the water goblet. Pour the first wine into the glass farthest to the right. Remove it from the table when you pour the next wine. Fill glasses half-full for dinner wines and one-third full for dessert and sparkling wines.

If you're serving more than one wine in the same glass, it is prudent to remove and rinse it out between each wine.

At the Table

If you open your wine at the table, cut neatly below the first ridge of the bottle's neck through the "capsule" (the metal or plastic cover over the cork) with a knife, wipe the mouth of the bottle with a clean napkin, then uncork the bottle. Unless you have some practice with other types of openers, choose a "wing type" (one with arms that go up and down)—it will make the job easier. Pour a bit into your glass first, taste it for flavor and temperature, then fill your guests' glasses no more than half full, allowing space to swirl the wine.

If you're serving from a decanter, there's no need to pour the first glassful. Simply urge your guests to help themselves and refill the decanter as needed.

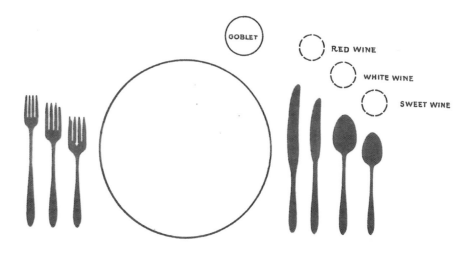

Decanting Your Wines

It is said that a good wine deserves decanting, and an ordinary wine requires it. Decanting is done for two reasons: to improve the appearance of a wine, and to bring out taste, aroma and bouquet. Older red wines (over ten years old) are often decanted to remove sediment, the microscopic particles of grapes that gradually settle to the bottom of the bottle during long storage. Young wines and white wines seldom have noticeable sediment, but their appearance can be enhanced by serving them in an attractive decanter.

Storing Leftover Wine

If you have dinner wine left, cork the bottle tightly and drink it the next day. For storage up to a week, decant to a smaller bottle to eliminate the air space above the wine and store in the refrigerator. Because of the higher alcoholic content, dessert wines will keep on the shelf or in the refrigerator for a month or two.

Don't subject leftover wines to multiple temperature changes. Choose one place for storage and keep wines there.

Barbecuing With Wine

Wine Marinades

What Do Marinades Do?

Marinating is a simple way to enhance the natural flavor of meat, fish, or poultry with wine, spices, and herbs. Because of the natural acidity in wine, wine marinades also help tenderize food. Extending marinating time will not totally tenderize meat for the tough connective tissue, collagen, can only be dissolved by heat.

Does Marinating Take Special Skill?

Most marinades are quite simple. Just place your meat, poultry, or fish in a glass or porcelain bowl. Pour enough wine over the meat to barely cover it. Add your choice of herbs and spices, cover the bowl, and let the marinade do the rest. All you have to do is turn the food occasionally with a wooden spoon. When the time is up, remove the food from the marinade, pat it dry with paper towels, and grill, bake, or sauté.

Which Wines Work Best?

Most dinner wines may be used for marinating. California Pinot Noir, Zinfandel, and Sauvignon Blanc are good choices. Wine left over from a recent meal makes an excellent marinade. Keep in mind that red wines will darken foods.

SUMMERTIME SANGRIA

1 bottle California Zinfandel or
   California Pinot Noir 750 ml
2 ounces brandy (optional)
1/4 cup sugar
1 lime, thinly sliced
1 lemon, thinly sliced
1 orange, thinly sliced
1/2 cup orange juice
1 cup club soda, chilled
Ice cubes

Combine wine, brandy, sugar, fruit, and juice in large pitcher. Refrigerate for 1 hour. Remove fruit to avoid bitterness. Add club soda at serving time and pour over ice cubes. Garnish with fresh seasonal fruit such as peaches, plums or strawberries. Makes 8 generous servings. (See page 26 for Strawberry Sangria)

In the sixties the winery introduced "Tingle," a popular aperitif wine and forerunner of the wine cooler. This lemon flavored white wine became an instant success.

How Long Should Foods Marinate?

Four or five hours is enough time for an average portion of meat or poultry (1 to 6 servings). Two hours is long enough for most fish. Food left in the marinade for longer periods does not become more tender. However, even a half hour of marinating will improve flavor. Meats may marinate at room temperature up to 2 hours; beyond that they should be refrigerated. Always refrigerate fish and poultry.

Should Marinades Be Saved?

Yes. Strain, refrigerate, and use within two weeks. Strained marinades may also be thickened with egg yolk or cornstarch, creating a sauce. Oils and butters may also be added to marinades, creating a baste for cooking.

BASIC MARINADE FOR RED MEATS:

This recipe has the basic ingredients of a tasty marinade. Try it—and then adjust it with your favorite herbs and spices.

1 carrot, thinly sliced
1 large onion, sliced
2 cloves garlic, crushed
Sprig parsley
2 stalks celery, sliced (optional)
6-8 peppercorns
1 bay leaf
1 whole clove
Pinch thyme
2-1/2 cups California Zinfandel

Mix all ingredients together then pour over red meat to barely cover.

DISCOVER ANCIENT MESQUITE

Grilling over mesquite charcoal is a tasty alternative to pan frying.

Mesquite wood, from the Sonoran desert of Mexico, has been used since ancient times for preparing meats. Settlers in the area first learned how to use it from the Indians living there.

Now, as modern cooks rediscover this venerable fuel, it has become available in food specialty shops and supermarkets.

Mesquite burns with a hotter flame than regular charcoal, so watch the trout carefully to avoid overcooking.

Because it contains no filler, as regular charcoal often does, mesquite imparts a delicious, natural wood smoke flavor that combines nicely with most marinades.

Using the hand crank, the family filled their vehicles with gas from an underground tank.

MARINADE FOR CHICKEN BREASTS

1/4 cup olive oil
1/4 cup soy sauce
1/4 cup Chardonnay wine
1/4 cup orange juice
1 onion, minced
2 cloves garlic, minced
1/4 teaspoon tarragon
1/4 teaspoon oregano
4 large bell peppers, cut into 2" pieces
4 chicken breasts cut into one-inch squares

Mix first 8 ingredients together. Add chicken pieces and marinade for one hour.

Place chicken breasts on skewer alternating with pieces of bell pepper. Place skewers over charcoal for approximately 20 minutes turning, frequently while adding additional marinade.

Gaspare and Sebastiano proudly posed in front of their flegling winery in 1948.

Basic Marinade for Poultry, Fish and White Meat

1 carrot, thinly sliced
1 large onion, sliced
1 clove garlic, crushed
1 teaspoon thyme
5 green onions, chopped
1 cup California Chardonnay wine
1/2 teaspoon salt
6 - 8 peppercorns
1 strip lemon peel

Combine all ingredients and marinate for two hours in the refrigerator, then grill or broil.

STRAWBERRY SANGRIA

1 cup strawberries, thinly sliced
1/2 cup sugar
1 whole lemon, thinly sliced
1 bottle California Chardonnay wine (750 ml)
2 cups club soda

In large bowl combine strawberries, sugar and lemon slices. Stir mixture, bruising the fruit lightly. Pour in wine, cover and chill at least 1 hour.
Remove lemon slices.

In punch bowl or large pitcher, blend wine mixture with club soda and pour over ice.
Serves 6.

(See page 23 for Summertime Sangria)

After the local high school football games my mother and father frequently hosted a group of schoolmates, family, neighbors, and friends. Mom always knew where the kids were when they were at her house eating and having a good time.
— Dorothy Indelicato

Appetizers

Biscotti

BISCOTTI

I was not only the oldest child, but the only girl as well. I learned to make Italian dishes such as biscotti by cooking alongside Mom every day.

Dad came from Campobello, Sicily while Mom and her sisters grew up in Moliterno, about thirty miles from Naples. When they married in this country, our kitchen became an Italian melting pot. Mom cooked some dishes her mother had taught her and some Sicilian recipes to please Dad. Pasta was the common denominator, of course.

We always ate the biscotti with coffee or wine. I love them with morning coffee, on the second day, when they're a bit dried out.

—Frances Indelicato Sciabica

6 cups flour, sifted
1-1/2 cups sugar
1-1/2 teaspoons salt
6 teaspoons baking powder
1/4 teaspoon black pepper
12 tablespoons shortening or 1-1/2 cubes butter
6 eggs, beaten
1/4 cup California brandy
1 egg yolk
2 tablespoons milk

Mix flour with sugar, salt, baking powder, and pepper. Spoon in shortening. Place eggs and brandy in center of mixture. Mix thoroughly.

Tear off enough dough to create a 1/2 x 6-inch "rope." Create a "doughnut" by joining ends.

Place dough circles on greased baking sheet. Mix egg yolk with 2 tablespoons milk and brush tops with egg wash. Bake 20 to 30 minutes at 350° until golden. Makes 2 dozen biscuits.

Wine Suggestion: California Riesling.

Three generations in 1961:
Vince, Robert at 4 years old,
and founder, Gaspare

Garlic Galore

Cooked garlic loses its punch, mellowing into a nutty sweetness. Keep the leftover garlic refrigerated in a covered jar. Add a clove or two to spaghetti sauce or vegetables.

3 tablespoons olive oil
3 tablespoons unsalted butter
6 heads garlic, tops removed, unpeeled
4 tablespoons California dry white wine
French bread slices, toasted

Heat oil and butter in a pan large enough to allow garlic heads to touch comfortably in one layer. Sauté garlic heads for several minutes, turning often until they are coated with butter and oil and tinged light brown.

Add wine and when it begins to boil, lower heat and simmer covered over until garlic is soft.

To serve, place hot garlic in a communal bowl and urge guests to help themselves. Pop softened garlic clove from skins and spread on toasted French bread. Enjoy with a bold red wine and goat cheeses.

Wine suggestion: California Petite Sirah or Zinfandel.

Antipasto Tray

Let guests linger over the antipasto course long enough for everyone to sample all the appetizing delicacies and become familiar with the hearty red wine chosen for this tasty medley.

Suggested Foods:
Caviar
Green onions
Small sardines in oil
Black and green olives
Tuna, canned or fresh ahi
Mortadella slices, rolled and fastened with toothpicks
Salami sliced very thin
Caponata (page 30)
Marinated mushrooms
Marinated artichokes
Parsley for garnish
Iceberg lettuce

Cover a large platter with lettuce leaves. Place tuna in center, arranging other foods around it in a sunburst design or arrange items in a striped effect around the plate. Tuck in parsley sprigs for garnish.

Mama and Papa with youngest son, Vincent in 1934.

Artichoke Bites

1 can artichoke hearts packed in water, drained (14 ounces)
1/3 cup California Sauvignon Blanc wine
1/4 cup finely grated Parmesan cheese
1/2 cup unseasoned bread crumbs
1/4 cup olive oil

Preheat oven to 400°. If using whole artichoke hearts, quarter or halve them into bite-size pieces. Soak in wine while preparing crumbs and cheese. Mix cheese and crumbs together in a dish. Place oil in a separate shallow dish. Lightly grease cookie sheet with vegetable oil or butter.

Remove artichoke pieces one at a time from wine. Shake gently, then dip into oil and roll lightly in crumb-cheese mixture. Place on cookie sheet about 1/2 inch apart.

Bake for 15 minutes or until lightly brown. Serve immediately with crisp whole wheat crackers. Makes about 32 quarter hearts.

Wine Suggestion: California Sauvignon Blanc or Chardonnay.

Richard's Lemon Shrimp

2 pounds medium to large shrimp, cooked, deveined with tail on
1/4 cup extra virgin olive oil
1/4 cup fresh lemon juice
1 bunch green onions (scallions), finely chopped
2 whole lemons, finely chopped
1/4 cup fresh cilantro, chopped
1/4 teaspoon salt
1/4 teaspoon pepper

Place shrimp in a large bowl. In a separate bowl, combine olive oil, chopped lemons, lemon juice, onions, cilantro, salt and pepper. Mix well and pour into bowl containing the shrimp. Chill for 6 hours.

Note: We make this recipe for our open house every holiday season. Guests love it.

Caterina's family, circa 1940.

Caponata

Wonderful, unusual flavors with a nice celery crunch. Chocolate mellows the mixture, but no one will guess it's there.

1 large eggplant cut into 1-inch cubes (about 3 cups)
1 tablespoon olive oil
3 cups celery, cut into 1/4-inch slices
1 tablespoon sugar
1½ teaspoons capers
2 tablespoons chopped black olives
2 tablespoons red wine vinegar
1½ teaspoons capers
1½ tablespoons grated, unsweetened chocolate
Salt and pepper

Peel eggplant and cut into 1-inch cubes. Sprinkle with salt and place on a plate. Put another plate over eggplant and weigh down to encourage weeping. Leave for 1 hour. Rinse eggplant pieces to remove salt and pat dry. Heat olive oil in skillet and fry eggplant until brown and soft. Remove and reserve.

    Add sliced celery to same pan and sauté until soft. Stir in eggplant, mixing well. Add sugar, capers, olives, vinegar and chocolate. Season with salt and pepper to taste. Mix well and chill. Serve as a vegetable side dish with cold meats or chicken. Also good on thin slices of French bread or unsalted crackers.

Wine Suggestion: California Zinfandel

Little Pizzas

1 can chopped black olives (4-1/2 ounces)
1 can chopped Ortega green chilies (4 ounces)
1 can tomato sauce (8 ounces)
3 to 4 garlic cloves, finely minced
4 cups grated sharp cheddar cheese
1/4 cup grated Romano cheese
2 French baguettes, sliced

Mix all ingredients. Spread on French bread slices and broil in toaster oven until mixture is bubbly.
Two French baguettes make approximately 80 bites. Recipe freezes well.

Every year, during our Manteca Holiday Open House, we serve about 1,000 Little Pizzas. I make the pizzas in the morning and put on trays of 30 pizzas each. These trays are placed in our walk-in refrigerator and taken out as we need them. The pizzas are cooked in small toaster ovens and served to guests "hot from the oven." Any left overs are enjoyed by staff the next day in our lunch room.

— Dorothy Indelicato

Spinach Squares

2 packages chopped frozen spinach (10 ounces each)
6 slices white bread, cut into 1/4-inch cubes
1/2 cup olive oil, don't substitute
1 cup milk
6 eggs, beaten
3 to 4 tablespoons dry minced onion
2 teaspoons Italian seasoning
1 teaspoon salt
1 teaspoon garlic powder
1 teaspooon black pepper
Paprika

Preheat oven to 350°. Cook spinach according to package directions and drain well. Combine with white bread cubes. Gradually add all ingredients (except paprika) in order of listing. Spread into greased 8x11-inch pan. Sprinkle generously with paprika. Bake 35 to 45 minutes at 350°. Let cool before cutting into 2 inch squares.

Wine Suggestion: California Zinfandel

Hint: Freeze bread slices for easier cutting.

Chicken Wings

Pick these up with your fingers and enjoy!

10 to 12 plump chicken wings
1/4 cup California cream sherry wine
1/4 cup light soy sauce
4 star anise pods
2 thin slices fresh ginger root

Rinse and dry chicken wings, then place in single layer under broiler. Broil until crisp, turning at least once. Wings should be almost completely cooked.

In flat skillet, combine sherry, soy sauce, anise pods and ginger. Bring to a boil, stirring continually. Reduce heat and add wings. Using tongs, turn over wings until well-coated and cook until they begin to glisten with soy mixture.

When liquid is almost absorbed, remove wings to heated platter. Serve immediately with plenty of paper napkins. The wings are also a wonderful picnic food, hot or cold. Serves two for dinner or several as an appetizer.

Wine Suggestions: California Chardonnay.

Sherried Walnuts

These crunchy sweet nuts require no cooking! Perfect as a topping for ice cream or a last minute hostess gift.

1-1/2 cups brown sugar
1/4 teaspoon salt
1/4 cup California dry sherry wine
2 tablespoons light corn syrup
3-1/2 cups walnut halves
Granulated sugar

Blend brown sugar, salt, sherry and corn syrup until smooth. Stir in walnuts, mixing until all are well-coated. Roll nuts in granulated sugar until lightly frosted. Place on waxed paper to dry.

Serve with a sip of sherry or a cup of strong coffee.

Cozzola

Ricotta Mixture:
2 pounds ricotta cheese (preferably fresh bulk)
1/4 cup sugar plus 4 tablespoons
3 tablespoons fresh parsley, chopped
1/2 teaspoon salt
2 egg yolks -- one beaten
4 hard-cooked eggs, thinly sliced
1 tablespoon cinnamon

Blend ricotta, sugar, parsley, salt, and egg yolk, then set aside.

PASTRY DOUGH:

5 cups flour
1/2 cup sugar
1/2 teaspoon salt
1 package dry yeast
1 tablespoon shortening
2 cups warm water—120° to 130°

Mix flour, sugar, salt and dry yeast then cut in shortening. Add warm water and blend well. Shape into balls, one slightly larger, and set aside in greased bowls, covered with a damp cloth, in a draft-free area until dough doubles in size.

Lightly flour rolling pin and surface. Roll larger dough ball into 1/2-inch thick rectangle. Lay in buttered 9 x 13-inch pan, bringing dough up sides of pan with 1/2-inch overlap.

Spread ricotta mixture on crust. Add sliced eggs on top. Mix cinnamon and sugar and sprinkle over eggs.

Roll out remaining dough. Lay on top of ricotta mixture and eggs, fluting it firmly together with bottom crust. Brush top with beaten egg yolk. Pierce top crust with fork. Bake 40 to 50 minutes at 350°. Cool at room temperature. Refrigerate until serving time. Makes 24 squares.

Wine Suggestion: California Riesling

COZZOLA

Cozzola was a special dish that we had at Easter and was from Mom's region of Italy. When we were small, Mom got the cheese from our neighbors and today I still make an effort to find fresh bulk ricotta. It makes a difference.
— Frances Indelicato Sciabica

Visiting Sicily in 1985.
Left -Right: Cousins, my son, Robert and me.

Castle Grammar School.
Vince in eighth grade -- 1947.

Carpaccio

An elegant first course that goes together in minutes.

1/2 pound lean, boneless, uncooked filet mignon, very thinly sliced*
4 anchovies, drained and minced
1/4 cup olive oil
2 tablespoons lemon juice
2 tablespoons capers
4 tablespoons white onion, minced
12 black olives
4 lemon wedges
Arugula greens and shaved parmesan cheese for garnish
French bread baguette, thinly sliced
Unsalted butter
Salt and pepper to taste

Divide meat slices among four plates. Place minced anchovies on top of meat. Combine olive oil with lemon juice and drizzle over each plate of beef. Make small mounds of capers and onions at the side of each plate, then garnish with black olives, shaved parmesan, lemon wedges and arugula greens.
Makes 4 servings.

Wine Suggestions: Serve with a robust California red wine such as
Petite Sirah or Cabernet Sauvignon.

Hint: Your butcher can slice the thinnest beef. If you're slicing it yourself, partially freeze the meat first.

We lived a simple life. Because we had little money, our daily meals were pretty much the same. We ate lots of bread. Every day at six o'clock in the morning, Muzio's bakery truck delivered ten loaves of crusty bread from Stockton.

For many years, eleven of us, six Indelicatos and five Luppinos, lived in the small frame house where there is now a parking lot.

Uncle, as we called Sebastiano Luppino, was the breakfast cook and he usually made us kids bacon and eggs. Sometimes, though, he'd fix eggs with home-cured black olives. Every day he'd say, "Breakfast ready. First call", like the porters on the trains he often rode to the East Coast to sell grapes.

If no one appeared, he'd say "Breakfast ready. Last call." When we finally stumbled sleepily into the kitchen the eggs were hard and cold, but they still tasted good to us.

-- Frances Indelicato Sciabica

Soups

Caterina's Minestrone

Lagrutta sisters: Caterina, Rosa, Virginia,1926.

After both parents died of smallpox, twenty-seven-year-old Elena traveled to Italy to bring Caterina, Serafina, Guiseppe, Rosa, and Virginia back to Lodi, California to live with her and her husband, Biaggio Albini. The siblings arrived at Ellis Island on December 31, 1920 aboard the S.S. America to begin their lives in the new country. The twins were twenty years old and Virginia, the youngest, was twelve. Giuseppe was seventeen and Rosa was thirteen.

For a short period of time they too joined the Indelicato/Luppino families, making a total of 14 people living in the four-bedroom house in Manteca.

—Vincent Indelicato

"It's the *fagioli romani* bean (Roman or cranberry bean) and the curly cabbage that make this soup so good," says Frances, who made it alongside her mother, Caterina Indelicato, for many years.

8 cups water
2 to 3 garlic cloves, minced
1 large onion, chopped fine
1/2 head celery, chopped
2 carrots, chopped
2 cups Swiss chard, coarsely chopped
1 zucchini, peeled and chopped
1/4 cup parsley, minced
4 or more fresh sweet basil leaves, minced
Pinch oregano
2 fresh tomatoes, skinned and crushed or 16 oz. can tomatoes with juice
Salt and pepper to taste
1 pound romani beans, cooked or 16 oz. can red kidney beans with juice
2 potatoes, cut into eighths
4 cups curly cabbage, coarsely chopped
3 tablespoons olive oil
1 cup uncooked elbow macaroni
Grated Romano cheese for serving

Boil water in a 6 to 8 quart kettle. Add garlic, onion, celery, carrots, Swiss chard, zucchini, parsley, sweet basil, oregano and tomatoes. Cover and simmer for 25 minutes.

Add salt, pepper and beans. Simmer 20 minutes. Next, add curly cabbage and olive oil. Cover and cook 20 minutes. Then add elbow macaroni and cook 10 more minutes.

Pass Romano cheese for those who wish to put some on top of the soup.
Serves 6 to 8.

Wine Suggestion: California Zinfandel.

Oyster Chowder

A hearty, creamy soup without a drop of cream.

4 tablespoons butter
3 tablespoons chopped onion
3/4 cup finely cut celery
3 carrots, finely diced
1/4 teaspoon thyme
1 cup California dry white wine
2 cups peeled, diced potatoes
1 quart milk, room temperature
1 pint oysters, reserve liquid
Salt and pepper to taste
1/3 cup minced parsley for garnish
Paprika

Melt butter in a saucepan and quickly sauté onion, celery and carrots for three minutes. Add oyster liquid, thyme, white wine and bring to a boil. Add potatoes, cover and simmer until tender. Add milk and bring just to the boiling point. Reduce heat, add oysters and cook until their edges curl. Salt and pepper to taste. Pour soup into bowls or a tureen and garnish with chopped parsley and paprika. Makes 4 meal-size servings.

Wine Suggestion: California Chardonnay.

Papa with sons Tony & Vince, 1936.

Consommé With Avocado

An elegant beginning for formal dinner parties and so easy to prepare.

2 cans beef broth (14-1/2 ounces each)
6 to 8 tablespoons California dry sherry wine
1 avocado, peeled and thinly cut into 1/2-inch pieces
2 small green onions, finely minced

Heat broth. Add sherry and simmer for 5 minutes. Divide avocado pieces equally among individual soup bowls. Sprinkle finely minced onions on soup and serve immediately with salted wheat crackers.
Serves 4 to 6.

Hint: Also a great take-along for picnics and sports events. Pour hot broth from thermos over diced avocado pieces in a mug.

Chilled Apricot Soup

1-1/2 cups canned, drained whole or half apricots*
3/4 cup California Moscato wine
1 cup natural unflavored yogurt
½ cup whole milk
Nutmeg

Purée apricots with wine in blender or food processor. Transfer to large bowl and whisk in yogurt and milk until smooth. Add more milk if necessary to please your taste. Refrigerate covered for at least 1 hour. Ladle soup into small bowls. Grate plenty of fresh nutmeg on surface of each serving. Serves 4 to 6.
   Combine with Oriental Chicken Salad (page 48) and popovers for an exotic lunch.

Wine Suggestion: California Pinot Grigio.

Fresh apricots may be substiuted and may require a small amount of sugar to be added.

Vince with first cousins in Campobello.
1975

Beef-Cheddar Chowder

1 pound ground beef
2 medium stalks celery, sliced (about 1 cup)
1 small onion, chopped
1 small green pepper, chopped
1/2 head cabbage, coarsely chopped
1/2 cup water
3 cups milk
2 cups shredded cheddar cheese
3 tablespoons flour
salt and pepper to taste
1/8 teaspoon ground nutmeg
2 tablespoons sliced pimiento

Cook and stir ground beef, celery, onion and green pepper in pot until vegetables are tender. Stir in cabbage and water. Cover and cook over low heat, stirring occasionally, until cabbage is done to your likeness, about 10 minutes.

Stir in milk, cheese, flour, salt, nutmeg and pepper. Heat to boiling, stirring constantly. Boil and stir 1 minute. Garnish each serving with pimento.
Serves 8.
Wine Suggestion: California Pinot Noir wine

Mushroom Soup

A creamy soup that boasts of fresh mushroom flavor.

1/2 pound fresh mushrooms, finely minced (about 2-1/2 cups)
1/2 cup finely minced onion
1 can chicken broth (14-1/2 ounces), heated
3 tablespoons butter plus 1 teaspoon
3 tablespoons flour
1-3/4 cups milk, heated
Salt and pepper to taste
1/4 cup California dry sherry wine
Nutmeg

Wipe mushrooms with a damp paper towel. Cut off stems, reserving four caps for garnish. Mince stems and remaining caps and add with onion to heated broth. Simmer uncovered for 30 minutes.

Slice and sauté remaining caps in 1 teaspoon butter and set aside. Melt 3 tablespoons butter in saucepan. Blend in flour until thick and smooth. Slowly add heated milk, whisking until sauce thickens. Stir thickened sauce into broth, stirring constantly. Taste for seasonings. Simmer for two minutes, continuing to stir. Add sherry and blend well. Ladle hot soup into 4 bowls, add sautéed mushrooms for garnish, grate nutmeg over top and serve immediately. Makes 4 soup servings or 2 hearty lunch portions.

This mushroom soup nicely introduces Easy Pork Chops With Fennel (page 111).

Wine Suggestion: California Sauvignon Blanc.

Francy made our lunches for school. As the only Indelicato daughter, she did a lot of work with Mom in the kitchen. Usually we had salami and cheese sandwiches on French bread. Some days, we had plain jelly sandwiches. We were embarrassed by the crusty, thick-sliced bread that labeled us as 'immigrant kids.' We were surprised, though, when the other kids offered to trade their bologna sandwiches made with thin-sliced white bread for our simpler ones.

When we came home hungry after school, we would barbecue homemade sausages on the coals of the pot-bellied wood stove and fill up on bread. At night we usually had soup, made with whatever was ripe in the garden.

We didn't have much red meat, because that had to be purchased. Instead, we ate lots of chicken and rabbits that we raised on the farm. We always butchered a hog for sausage and other pork dishes. We were pretty much self-sufficient. There were plenty of vegetables in our garden, so we always ate three good meals a day, even when times were tough.

By the time we boys were ready to attend college, we thought the food at home was pretty ordinary. We were mighty tired of spaghetti and minestrone. But a few weeks of cafeteria food changed all that. On our first visit home, we ate everything in sight.

—Vincent Indelicato

The children of founders, 1934.
Back: Antonio, Sam, Frances, Frank. Front: Tony, Vince.

I grew up on this hearty, simple Portuguese soup, and now my family loves it, too.

My father, Joe Cardoza, who emigrated from the Azores and my mother, Mary, early in their married life lived on property adjoining the Indelicato land.

My mother remembered meeting Gaspare across the fence. She and my father were young, newly married and Gaspare took them under his wing. He'd come to visit, always bringing whatever he had extra from his garden. At Christmas he brought them a gallon of wine.

One day, my dad recalled, Gaspare came over to ask if he could buy a cow to supply milk for his family. My dad explained to him about the cost of hay and veterinary bills, even for one cow. Gaspare listened and reasoned it wasn't economical. Instead he bought milk from my folks who had a dairy farm. That was good for both families.

In 1954 Gaspare's son, Vince and I were married.

--Dorothy Indelicato

Vince and Dorothy with their wedding party, 1954

Kale Soup

Caldo Verde

2-1/2 to 3 pounds beef with bones
2-1/2 quarts cold water
Salt and pepper
1 medium onion, chopped
1 tablespoon minced parsley
4 large potatoes, quartered
5 cups kale (or chard), loosely packed, ribs removed
1 tablespoon wine vinegar
1 can mixed vegetables

Place meat in cold water with salt, pepper, onions and parsley. Simmer for 3 hours. Remove meat and bones. Add potatoes and kale and simmer for 45 minutes. Return meat, add vinegar and mixed vegetables and serve immediately.
Serves 6

Kale Soup -- Marie's Version

1 - 2 pounds beef with bones
1 tablespoon olive oil
1 small yellow onion, chopped
1 teaspoon garlic, chopped
1 cup celery, inside ribs with leaves, cut into small pieces
1/2 cup California red wine
14 cups cool water
1 can tomato sauce (8 oz.)
2 teaspoons Italian seasoning
2 teaspoons parsley, dried
1 tablespoon salt
5 cups kale, coarsely chopped, large ribs removed
1 medium potato, peeled and cut into small pieces
1/2 cup white rice

Brown the meat in olive oil then add onions, garlic and celery. Sauté until vegeables are soft and a bit carmelized. Pour in red wine and scrape bottom of pot to loosen crunchy bits. Add water, tomato sauce, Italian seasonings, parsley and salt. Simmer covered for two hours.

Increase heat to medium and bring to a rolling boil. Add kale, potatoes and rice. Reduce heat and simmer covered for 30 - 45 minutes, until all are cooked well. Serve hot with grated parmesan cheese if desired. Serves 6

Hint: This soup can easily become vegetarian-friendly. Omit the meat and replace 6 cups of water with 6 cups of vegetable broth.

40

Wine Suggestion: California Chardonnay

Zucchini Bread

Frank and Alice Indelicato's daughter, Cheryl, likes to cook nutritious foods. Her brother, Michael, always has a big garden and in this recipe she uses some of his abundant summer zucchini.

1 cup oil
2 cups sugar
3 eggs, beaten
2 cups grated fresh zucchini or one, 16oz package of frozen sliced
    zucchini, defrosted and run through food processor
2 cups flour
1/2 teaspoon baking powder
2 teaspoons baking soda
1 teaspoon salt
2 to 3 teaspoons cinnamon
1 cup coarsely chopped walnuts
2 teaspoons vanilla

Blend oil, sugar and eggs. Add zucchini. Sift dry ingredients together and add to zucchini mixture. Stir in nuts. Add vanilla and mix well. Pour into 2 lightly greased loaf pans. Bake 50 to 60 minutes at 350°. Cool 10 minutes before removing from pans.

Hint: Cheryl suggests that when zucchini is plentiful, grate it and freeze in 2-cup portions, then defrost it any time of the year to bake this tasty bread.

Pea Soup

2 cups split peas (1 lb. pkg. of green or yellow peas)
1 ham hock or 3 slices of 1/2 inch crispy bacon
1 medium onion, chopped
2 ribs of celery. chopped
2 cloves of garlic, chopped
2 bay leaves
6 cups water
1 teaspoon salt (or to taste)
1/2 teaspoon pepper

Wash and clean peas of any foreign materials. Rinse peas. In a medium sized pan, add peas, water, onion, ham hock, celery, garlic, and bay leaves. Cover and bring to a boil. Simmer for about one hour, stirring about every fifteen minutes or until peas are tender. Add additional water if needed. Remove bay leaves, add salt and pepper. Serve hot with French bread.

Wine Suggestion: California Merlot or Pinot Noir

Cheryl & Dorothy Indelicato.

POPOVERS

1 cup milk
2 eggs
1 cup all-purpose flower
1/2 teaspoon of salt

Heat oven to 450°. Generously grease 6-cup popover (cupcake) pan and place the pan in the oven for 5 minutes.

Meanwhile, heat milk in microwave, uncovered, on high until warm. Beat eggs slightly in a medium bowl and then stir in flour, milk and salt. Beat with a fork or wire whisk until smooth, making sure not to overbeat the mixture. Fill pan cups half full and bake for 20 minutes.

Reduce the even temperature to 350° and bake for 15-20 minutes longer, or until golden brown. Immediately remove popovers from pan. Serve warm.

Great with Pear and celery soup.
(See page 44)

California Onion Soup

A delicate, cream-colored soup with a mild onion flavor. Everyone who tastes it will ask for the recipe.

The Indelicato and Luppino families were making a living on the land until Prohibition ended in 1933. Then customers in the East no longer needed grapes for home winemaking. Dad couldn't even get five dollars a ton for them.

There were other small vineyards around us, owned mostly by Italian immigrants, too. When things got tough, a lot of the farmers plowed under their vines and planted other crops or left the area. Some of our nieghbors had tanks they weren't using and one day Dad and Uncle said, "Let's make wine!"

- Frank Indelicato

3 large yellow onions, thinly sliced (about 6 cups)
6 tablespoons butter
3 cans chicken broth (14-1/2 ounces each)
1-1/2 cups California Sauvignon Blanc wine
Salt and pepper
6 slices French bread
1-1/2 cups coarsely grated Swiss cheese

Sauté onions in butter until soft and transparent. Be careful to avoid browning. Add broth and simmer until it is reduced by one-third. Add wine, salt and pepper. Bring to a boil once more and simmer for 10 minutes. Lightly toast 1-inch thick slices of French bread. Place one in each soup bowl. Top with 1/4 cup grated Swiss cheese. Ladle steaming soup over both. Serves 4 to 6.

A good soup choice to introduce Baked Ham In Wine (page 110).

Wine Suggestion: California Sauvignon Blanc

Gaspare relaxes after a long day in the field.
He had just learned his friend, Peter Busalacchi, helped him get a loan from the
Bank of Stockton. Peter helped save the ranch from foreclosure.

Spinach Soup

Your guests will love this interesting soup, even if they don't believe the main ingredient is spinach.

1/2 pound fresh spinach or one, 8 oz package frozen spinach, thawed
1 tablespoon vegetable oil
2 tablespoons finely minced fresh ginger
2 green onions, chopped, including some greens
2 cans chicken broth (14-1/2 ounces each)
1/4 cup California dry sherry wine
2 teaspoons soy sauce
1/4 cup sour cream
Sour cream for garnish

Wash spinach and strip from stems. Heat oil. Sauté ginger for about 1 minute. Add spinach and onions, stirring 2 to 3 minutes. Add broth, sherry and soy sauce. Bring to a boil, then simmer for 10 minutes.

Purée with 1/4 cup sour cream. Stir well and chill thoroughly or serve hot. Garnish with a dollop of sour cream. Makes 4 petite servings or 2 meal-size portions.

Serve with Spoon Bread.

Wine Suggestion: California Sauvignon Blanc.

Spoon Bread

3 eggs, separated
3 cups milk
1 cup yellow or white cornmeal
1 cup milk
1 teaspoon salt
1 teaspoon baking powder
1 tablespoon butter

Beat egg whites until stiff and set aside. In large pan, scald 3 cups milk. In a bowl, mix cornmeal with 1 cup cold milk and stir into scalded milk. Continue heating over medium heat, stirring constantly. Stir yolks into cornmeal mixture. When mixture thickens, remove from heat and add salt, baking powder, and butter. Fold in egg whites.

Grease 2-quart casserole. Pour in mixture and bake at 350° for 50 minutes or until browned on top. Serve immediately. Serves 4 to 6.

Angelo Rolleri, who knew Gaspare Indelicato and his family, came to America from Italy in 1914. Four years later he opened Genova Bakery to make bread the European way. Today, the bread is still rolled by hand and baked to golden crispness in the specially built brick oven. Special occasions in the Stockton area call for Genova bread on the table. At the Indelicato family sausage making evenings, there are always plenty of loaves to enjoy.

As Angelo grew older, he turned the breadmaking over to younger bakers, but he still sat every day in the same spot, on an old wine box, greeting regular customers and neighbors until his death in 1985.

--- Frank Indelicato

Angelo Rolleri of Genova Bakery,
Stockton California

Pear And Celery Soup

2-3/4 cups finely chopped celery
2 cans chicken broth (14-1/2 ounces each)
1 cup peeled, chopped Bartlett pear
1/3 cup California Chardonnay wine
2 tablespoons heavy cream
Nutmeg

Simmer celery and broth uncovered for about 20 minutes or until celery is soft. Puree celery and pear in blender, gradually adding hot broth. Add wine. Chill.

At serving time, stir well and ladle into serving bowls. Carefully top with cream and a grating of nutmeg.
Serves 6.

Accompany with popovers (page 41), Peppery Kebabs (page 96), Vegetable Kebabs (page 122), and Spanish Basque Flan (page 132) for a wonderful meal all within the pages of this book.

Wine Suggestion: Gewürztraminer or California Chardonnay.

ROYAL RED
1 teaspoon cherry liqueur
1 teaspoon lemon juice
1 teaspoon powdered sugar
2/3 cup California Pinot Noir wine
Cracked ice
Fresh fruit

Make a syrup by mixing liqueur, juice and sugar in a tall glass. Add Pinot Noir and cracked ice. Garnish with fruit. Makes a single serving.

Apple Lemon Soup

Wonderful fresh-apple flavor with a texture like delicate apple sauce.

5 to 6 medium apples (1-1/2 pounds)
1 cinnamon stick
1 lemon rind, cut into strips
3 tablespoons cornstarch
1/2 cup water
1/4 cup sugar
1/2 teaspoon salt
1/2 cup California Pinot Grigio wine
Sour cream

Core apples and cut each into 6 pieces. Place in deep kettle with 1-1/2 quarts water, cinnamon stick, and lemon rind. Cook over low heat until apples are very soft. Remove cinnamon and purée lemon rind and apples with liquid. Return to kettle.

Blend cornstarch in water and stir into soup. Cook over low heat until thickened and smooth, stirring constantly. Add sugar, salt and wine. Serve hot or cold with a dollop of sour cream. Serves 6.

Wine Suggestion: California Pinot Grigio.

Salads

Little Caesar Salad

1 large head broccoli
1 large head Romaine lettuce
1/2 cup olive oil
1/3 cup California dry white wine
2 tablespoons white wine vinegar
1/2 teaspoon salt
Freshly ground pepper
1/4 teaspoon Worcestershire sauce
Dash paprika
1/3 cup grated Parmesan cheese
1 minced garlic clove
1 raw egg yolk (optional)
Minced anchovies (optional)

In 1926, after leveling the land, Dad and Uncle Sam Luppino planted small plots of Carignane, Mission and Zinfandel grapes for making their own wine. They sold the excess grapes to East Coast home winemakers.

The walnut trees were planted at the ends of the vineyards so Dad and Uncle had a shady place to rest the horses. Just recently when we planted new vines we knew it would be practical to uproot the trees and make room for additional vines. But we all decided we needed these trees for sentiment's sake. It was here under these trees that Dad and Uncle sat and drilled each other in English. Dad was determined to learn English so that he could respond to the judge when he went to get his citizenship papers. "The judge said the questions and I answered right back. The judge said nice words about my answers," he remembered proudly.

—Vince Indelicato

Wash broccoli, removing flowerettes and chopping thin stems into 1/2-inch pieces. Use thick stalks for other purposes. Steam until al dente. Cool.

Wash and dry Romaine leaves. Wrap loosely in paper towels if salad will not be prepared immediately.

Combine remaining ingredients, except egg yolk and anchovies, in mixing bowl and beat until well-blended. Pour slowly over lettuce and broccoli, stopping when mixture is moist, not soaking. (You may have more dressing then necessary for this salad. Use the rest as a marinade for meat or chicken.) Toss lightly. Drop in egg yolk and add anchovies, if desired.

If dressing will not be used immediately, store in covered container in refrigerator and beat well just before serving.
Serves 4

A = Barn turned winery
B = Winery sales room
C = Gaspare's garden
D = House where families lived
E = Rabbit hutch/Chicken coup
F = Walnut trees
G = Vineyards

46

Tossed Spinach Salad

This crisp and fresh salad goes with many entrées. It's delicious as a luncheon salad.

8 water chestnuts, thinly sliced
3 hard-cooked eggs, thinly sliced
3 slices bacon, finely crumbled
1/4 cup oil
1 tablespoon sugar
1 tablespoon catsup
1 tablespoon white wine vinegar
1/2 teaspoon Worcestershire sauce
2 teaspoons California dry sherry wine
1 large bunch spinach
2 green onions, coarsely chopped, including some greens
3 cups bean sprouts
Black pepper to taste

Vince and his cousin inspecting the family's vineyards in Campobello, Sicily, in 1975.

If you have time, crispen chestnuts by draining water from can and refilling with tap water mixed with 1 teaspoon sugar. Refrigerate until using. Keep unused chestnuts in sugar solution until needed.

Boil eggs until hard-cooked. Cool and set aside. Fry bacon slices until crisp. Drain on absorbent paper. Crumble or cut into small pieces. Set aside.

Combine oil, sugar, catsup, vinegar, Worcestershire sauce and sherry. Shake well in jar.

Wash spinach and destem. Dry with towel or spin dry. Place in large bowl. Add onions and bean sprouts. Toss lightly but well.

Add dressing and toss again. Season with pepper to taste. Slice eggs and lay on top. Serve immediately.

Makes 6 side salads or 4 entrée salads.

Wine Suggestion: California Viognier.

Scene from Campobello, Sicily in 1985.

Oriental Chicken Salad

GLISTENING RICE

2 cups boiling water
1 cup rice
1/4 cup white vinegar
3 teaspoons sugar
1/2 teaspoon salt

Add rice to boiling water. Bring to boil and stir. Reduce heat to lowest flame and cover pot. Cook without lifting lid for 20 minutes. Turn off heat and let sit for 5 minutes.

Place hot rice in bowl. Combine vinegar, sugar, and salt and pour mixture over rice. Stir thoroughly. Let cool to room temperature. Cover and chill.

At serving time, pack rice into small bowls (about 1/2 cup capacity). Unmold on center of individual plates. Arrange salad around mound. Serves 4.

This salad has several preparation stages but the beautiful blend of flavors makes it all worthwhile. Most of this salad can be prepared the day before and the chilled ingredients assembled in minutes, just before serving.

2 chicken breasts or 2 cups chicken meat
Chicken marinade
1 cup walnut pieces
Dash salt
1 teaspoon curry powder
12 ounces Chinese pea pods
3 cups watercress, without stems
Salad Dressing
Glistening Rice

CHICKEN MARINADE:

1/3 cup soy sauce
1/3 cup California dry sherry wine
4 garlic cloves
4 thin slices fresh ginger

Marinate chicken 1 to 2 hours in the refrigerator. Broil until done and skin is crisp. Slice meat into thin strips. Reserve and chill.

WALNUTS:

Place nuts on cookie sheet or tin foil in 300° oven. Sprinkle with salt and 1 teaspoon curry powder. Toast until crisp and lightly brown. Cool nuts for at least an hour, allowing them to become crisp before adding to salad.

PEA PODS:

Rinse pods and remove strings. Blanch in boiling water for 2 to 3 minutes until just barely cooked. Submerge immediately in ice water to retain crispness. Drain and chill.

WATERCRESS:

Wash watercress. Remove thick stems. Divide into small sprigs but do not cut or mince. Shake dry and wrap in cloth or paper towel. Refrigerate.

SALAD DRESSING:

5 tablespoons peanut oil
3 tablespoons white vinegar
1/2 teaspoon mild curry powder

Mix thoroughly and reserve. Shake well before adding to salad minutes before serving.

SERVING:

At serving time combine watercress, pea pods, chicken and nuts. Toss well. Add salad dressing and toss lightly. Surround Glistening Rice with salad.

Wine Suggestion: California Viognier.

Gaspare and Caterina, 1931.

Scallop Salad

A delicate crunch of cucumber and nuts plus summer colors of pink and green. Gorgeous presented in a clear glass bowl.

1 cup California dry white wine
Bouquet garni of 1/4 teaspoon thyme, 2 sprigs parsley,
   2 pieces green onion (1 inch long), 1 bay leaf
1 pound bay scallops (the tiny ones)
6 tablespoons grapeseed oil
1 tablespoon white wine vinegar
1/4 teaspoon mustard
8 tablespoons peeled, finely minced cucumber
4 tablespoons minced pistachios
Parsley
Salt to taste
Bibb lettuce or watercress
Lime wedges for garnish

Bring wine to a simmer, add bouquet garni and poach scallops for 5 minutes. Cool. Remove scallops from liquid.

   Mix grapeseed oil, vinegar and mustard. Marinate scallops in mixture in the refrigerator for at least 2 hours.

   At serving time, add cucumber, pistachios, parsley and salt, and mix well.

   Serve in a single Bibb lettuce leaf or in a nest of watercress. Add 2 lime wedges for each serving. Serves 4.

Wine Suggestion: California Chardonnay.

Minted Tomato Salad

SALAD DRESSING:

4 tablespoons olive oil
2 tablespoons California dry white wine
1 teaspoon lemon juice
Freshly ground black pepper
Dash cayenne pepper
Pinch sugar
Pinch dry mustard
1 clove garlic, crushed

Blend all ingredients. Remove garlic clove and chill 1 hour
before serving.

SALAD:

6 firm tomatoes, skinned and sliced
1 medium onion, thinly sliced
1 cup fresh mint leaves, finely minced
Salad dressing
Romaine lettuce

Combine tomatoes, onions and mint in a bowl. Pour dressing over all and
toss lightly. Serve on crisp lettuce leaves. Delicious with grilled lamb.
Serves 6

Wine Suggestion:: California Merlot.

Vince & Tony discussing issues of the day at The Stockton Symphony Fundraiser in 2002.

French Potato Salad

6 medium potatoes
1/8 teaspoon salt
1/8 teaspoon freshly ground pepper
3 tablespoons tarragon or white wine vinegar*
2 tablespoons chicken broth
2 tablespoons California dry white wine
1 teaspoon dried tarragon
1 tablespoon fresh parsley
3 tablespoons salad oil (not olive oil)

Cook potatoes in salt water for 30 minutes or until tender. Peel while still warm and cut into slices approximately 1/4-inch thick. Place in bowl.

In smaller bowl, combine salt, pepper, vinegar, broth and wine. Mix until salt is dissolved. Add tarragon and parsley. Whisk in oil. Pour over warm potatoes. Toss gently until all liquid is absorbed. Serve while warm.
Makes 6 servings.

This dish is a natural contribution to a picnic. Delicious with sweet and sour carrots, pumpernickel bread, and corned beef.

Hint: Potatoes should absorb the flavorings while they are still warm—otherwise they get a "cold potato" taste which overpowers the delicate dressing.

Wine Suggestion: California Sauvignon Blanc.

Do not use red wine vinegar. If using plain cider or white wine vinegar without tarragon, increase dried tarragon by 1/4 teaspoon.

Vacations were almost unheard of for a large family like ours in the Depression days, but we did have a chance to go camping near Chico, at Richardson Springs. We had very little money to spend, just enough for the gas to get there.

There were seven of us in a 1935 Chevy. People used to count in disbelief as we got out of that small car, one by one.

Because we had no cash for groceries, we took along our food, including a crate of live chickens. We must have made quite a sight all packed in the car like sardines, and those squawking chickens tied on the back. When we got there, they crowed at sunrise and woke up our family and everyone else.
—Vincent Indelicato

Some of these chicken came along with us on our vacation.

We all piled in this car for our vaction -- :
Mom, Dad, Frank, Tony, Vince and
our neighbors, Vito and Teresa Bianco

Chick Pea Salad

In May 1935, the winery officially opened. Proud to be in business in this new land, Dad and Uncle, partners in this new venture, Americanized their names: Sebastiano became Sam, and Gaspare changed to Jasper. They called their venture the Sam Jasper Winery.

The winery's first vintage, 3,451 gallons, was made in a converted hay barn, using a small hand crusher and a hand-operated winepress. Local people, mostly Italians, bought the red wine that first year for 50 cents a gallon.

We did everything ourselves—growing the grapes, making the wine and selling it.

—Frank Indelicato

This is a recipe from Joe Larranaga, Delicato employee for 25 years. Joe recommended this bean dish either as a salad or as a side dish with meat, fish or chicken. "The Basques make a fine sandwich of these beans and French bread," Joe added.

1 pound dried garbanzo beans
1 teaspoon salt
1 medium onion, minced
2 cloves garlic, minced
2 tablespoons tomato sauce
1 tablespoon olive oil

Wash the garbanzos and put them in a deep kettle with salt and enough water to cover. Soak overnight. Add more water if necessary to cover beans completely.

Bring to a boil, skimming off foam 3 or 4 times until water is clear. Add minced onion and garlic, tomato sauce and oil. Cover and simmer for 3 hours. Refrain from stirring bean but check often to maintain enough liquid. Makes four dinner or eight salad portions.

Wine Suggestion: California Cabernet Sauvignon

Enjoying dinner with Gaspare's sisters and their families in Sicily 1975.

Basic Vinaigrette

Also called basic French dressing. The usual proportion of vinegar to oil is 1 to 3, but you may want to discover your own ratio.

1/2 cup olive oil
2 tablespoons red wine vinegar
2 tablespoons Zinfandel
1/2 teaspoon salt
Freshly ground black pepper

Put ingredients in a small bowl. Stir until salt dissolves.

Hints: For all green salads, be certain leaves are completely dry so dressing will adhere. Toss salad just before serving time and add only enough dressing to coat the leaves. There should be no pool of dressing left in the bottom of the bowl.

Newly purchased in 1998, Merlot grape vines were planted at Clay Station in Lodi, California.

Additions to Basic Vinaigrette:

• Add 1/2 teaspoon mustard, 1/2 teaspoon Worcestershire sauce and one minced clove garlic.

• Add 3 teaspoons chopped anchovies, 1-1/2 teaspoons chopped capers, teaspoons chopped parsley and 4 drops Tabasco sauce.

• Add 1 teaspoon sugar and a pinch each of dried basil and tarragon.

• Add 3 tablespoons chutney, 2 teaspoons A1 Steak Sauce and 1 tablespoon dried chervil.

• Add 1/4 cup total combination or single selection of fresh herbs: marjoram, rosemary, tarragon, parsley, chives or mint.

Vineyard Vinaigrette

Newborn Camdan Indelicato is welcomed
by Vince and Jeanette at the
2004 Sausage Party.

6 tablespoons grapeseed oil
3 tablespoons red wine vinegar
1 tablespoon honey
1 clove garlic, peeled and crushed
1/8 teaspoon tarragon
1/8 teaspoon basil
1/8 teaspoon oregano

Mix all ingredients together thoroughly. Let sit at least 30 minutes, removing garlic
at that time if dressing will be stored longer. Shake well before pouring over lettuce
greens. Makes approximately 1/2 cup dressing.

White Wine Dressing

6 tablespoons olive oil
2 tablespoons California dry white wine
1/2 teaspoon lemon juice (optional)
1/2 teaspoon salt
Freshly ground pepper
Dash cayenne pepper
Pinch sugar
Pinch dry mustard
One mild onion sliced

Blend ingredients together and let rest for at least 30 minutes. Remove onion slice
before serving.

Pasta

Tips For The Best Pasta

Pasta is more than spaghetti Pasta comes in rings, shells, strands, elbows, tubes—even mustache shapes! Team up any of these with pasta sauces for an exciting new dinner time combination.

Allow 4 ounces of dried pasta for each guest. Serve cooked pasta in a large bowl in the center of the table or dish up individual portions from the head of the table.

Place bowls of freshly grated parmesan or Romano cheeses, sweet butter, minced parsley, green onions, grated walnuts, pesto, and anchovies on the table. Diners can spice up sauces with these condiments or create their own flavor combinations.

Red or White Wine With Pasta?

If your pasta sauce is abundantly flavored with garlic, herbs and tomato, try a hearty red wine such as Zinfandel or Petite Sirah. If your sauce is more delicate or you prefer white wine, serve a full-bodied white, such as Chardonnay or Sauvignon Blanc.

For The Best Possible Pasta:

• Cook in plenty of water. Use 3 quarts of water for each 8 ounces of dried pasta (two average servings). Bring water to a rolling boil. Slowly add pasta. Bring to a second boil, and simmer until done.

• Do not overcook. Chefs agree that the cooking times given on pasta packages are too long. Pasta tastes best al dente (tender but firm "to the tooth"). Spaghetti is well-cooked in 12 minutes and smaller pasta pieces even faster. Taste a piece as cooking time nears 10 minutes.

• Do not rinse cooked pasta. Pasta has a better texture if it is not rinsed. Lift pasta directly from cooking water to serving plate or bowl with a pasta fork or other utensil. Drain smaller pasta in a colander.

• Adding olive oil will keep pasta from sticking.

• Keep plenty of pasta in your cupboard and sauce in your freezer and you'll always have quick, tasty meals near at hand.

In 1948 very few cars traveled the old highway. (It is now a six lane freeway). Notice the sign that reads El Dorado Motel. In those days it was unusual to have travelers' rooms cooled.

In 1935 the road in front of the winery was called North Manteca Road.

Anchovy Sauce

1/4 cup olive oil
4 tablespoons butter
4 garlic cloves, minced
1 can anchovies (2 ounces) drained and minced
1/4 cup California dry white wine
1/3 cup minced parsley

Heat olive oil and butter. Add garlic and cook over low heat until garlic is soft but not brown. Add anchovies and wine and mix well. Stir until anchovies blend into the sauce. Add parsley and serve immediately over hot pasta. Makes about 3/4 cup sauce.

Today's Tomato Sauce

We name this recipe "today's tomato sauce" because it shows a change from the original recipe which called for home canned tomatoes grown in the garden. "Now we use commercially canned tomato sauce, but cook it the same way," says Frances, who believes that 30 minutes is the most time needed to simmer a sauce.

This basic sauce is delicious over pasta and if added by the spoonful will enhance other sauces.

Frances remembers, too, when a whole head of garlic would be dropped in the sauce and cooked until soft. In Italian, garlic is called a "lamb's head" and would be divided between the servings.

"Or, if you like a thick sauce," Frances says, "put a cut-up, raw potato in the sauce and cook it until it is done."

3 tablespoons olive oil
3/4 cup finely minced onions
4 cloves garlic, minced
3 cans tomato sauce (8 ounces each)
Salt and pepper to taste
Bay leaf

Brown onions and garlic in olive oil. Add tomato sauce, bay leaf and salt and pepper. Simmer for 30 minutes.

Caterina's Pasta Ascuitta

CATERINA'S SUNDAY NIGHT PASTA ASCUITTA

Every Sunday night we ate pasta ascuitta, which means pasta with sauce. The pasta could be any shape—whatever Mom bought at the Italian grocery in town but the sauce was usually the same. We ate as much as our stomachs could hold. It was contentment. We could even forget we had to go to school the next day.

—Frank Indelicato

All four Indelicato children remember the good pasta with sauce that the family ate every Sunday night. Frances, because she cooked alongside her Mom, remembers how it was prepared. Today, Frances sometimes substitutes beef for poultry. "Just be sure the beef is cooked through before adding the other ingredients," she advises.

Olive oil for frying
1 rabbit or chicken, cut up into small pieces
3 garlic cloves, minced
3/4 cup minced onion
Salt and pepper to taste
1 can whole tomatoes with juice (28 ounces)
2 cans tomato sauce (8 ounces each)
1 can tomato paste (2 ounces)
1/4 cup minced parsley
Fresh sweet basil to taste, minced
Pasta (Spaghetti, Linguini, Mostaccioli or your choice)
Grated Romano cheese

In a 6 to 8 quart saucepan heat olive oil. Brown chicken or rabbit pieces for about 20 minutes with lid on. Add garlic, onion and salt and pepper and simmer covered for 10 to 15 minutes. Add tomatoes, tomato sauce and paste, parsley and basil. Simmer covered for 45 minutes.

Serve hot over cooked pasta. Place a bowl of grated cheese on the table so guests can sprinkle some on top. This recipe will feed 4 to 8, depending on the size of appetites. It can easily be expanded by adding another can of tomatoes and cutting poultry into smaller pieces.

The Indelicato Family, 1975.

Sciabica's Pasta Topping

Joe Sciabica fixed up a batch of this pasta topping for himself and son, Joe, Jr. when their wives, Frances and Laurie, were gone for the evening. Joe didn't worry too much about the ratio of ingredients. "It's how you want it, and all you want," laughed Joe.

1/2 cup bread crumbs*
1 or 2 garlic cloves, minced
3 leaves sweet basil, minced
3 sprigs parsley, finely minced
2 tablespoons Romano or Parmesan cheese
1 tablespoon olive oil
1/4 pound pasta of your choice

Mix bread crumbs, garlic, basil, parsley and cheese. Blend in olive oil and mix well. Place mixed bread crumbs in heavy skillet over low heat. Stir constantly with wooden spoon so mixture will not burn. When crumbs are toasted, remove from heat.

In a separate pot cook pasta. Drain the pasta but reserve about 1/4 cup of cooking water. Return it to the pasta so it won't be dry. Add the toasted bread crumbs and toss lightly. Sprinkle cheese on top and dig in! Makes two people very content.

Added Joe, "I nuke my own bread crumbs from hard French bread. Or, if I don't have bread on hand, I use Progresso Bread Crumbs Italian-Style and simply add the olive oil."

Joe Sciabica, Sr., son-in-law of founder, enjoying his wine, 1985.

Mushroom Sauce

1-1/2 pounds mushrooms, very thinly sliced
1/2 cup butter
2/3 cup California dry white wine
1 garlic clove, crushed
1/2 cup minced parsley
6 ounces cooked pasta
Black pepper, freshly ground

Sauté mushrooms in butter in shallow skillet until they are golden and the mushroom liquid disappears (about 20 minutes).

Add wine and garlic and simmer, occasionally stirring. When wine is almost completely gone, remove from heat and add parsley. Add cooked, hot pasta and toss together. Grind black pepper over all. Makes 2 dinner servings or 4 first-course servings.

Spaghetti Ragu

My children went to the winery with me every morning. Around 9:30, the time Nanna Indelicato usually ate breakfast, the children went next door to see her and have a second breakfast. Robert, now owner of a 90 acre vineyard and a wine broker, still remembers how Nanna cooked the eggs fresh from the backyard chickens. "They were soft," he recalls. He and his sister, Marie, would dip their French bread slices into the yolk of the eggs. "No eggs have ever tasted as good since," they claim.

After their second breakfast with Nanna, the children joined me in the office, sometimes playing under my desk, crouching by my feet. When they were older they told me how they'd stay quiet and watch the feet on the other side of the desk when I had a visitor.

I often prepare pasta because Vince enjoys it so much. When the children were young they were always hungry and couldn't wait for dinner. I could satisfy them temporarily by dipping pieces of French bread in the simmering sauce until their father returned from work to have dinner. They still talk about my good before-dinner snacks.

– Dorothy Indelicato

1 pound lean ground beef
1/2 cup finely minced onion
2 cloves garlic, minced
5 cans tomato sauce (8 ounces each)
1 sprig fresh rosemary (or 1/4 teaspoon dried)
1 tablespoon fresh, minced parsley
1/2 teaspoon thyme
1 large bay leaf
1 teaspoon dried oregano
1/2 cup California dry red wine
Salt
Mushrooms, sliced (optional)
4 ounces spaghetti per serving

Brown beef in skillet until almost cooked. Leave about 2 tablespoons fat in pan with meat. Sauté onions and garlic until limp. Add tomato sauce, mushrooms, herbs and wine. Salt to taste. Stir well. Bring to a boil. Turn heat down to simmer. Cook 30 minutes to an hour. Remove the bay leaf.

Makes enough sauce for 8 servings.

Vermicelli With Mint

Begin a summer meal with small portions of this pasta, followed by Roast Chicken (page 77) and Red Pepper Gratin (page 120).

3 tablespoons butter
2 cloves garlic, crushed
1/2 pound mild Italian sausage
1/2 cup California dry white wine
1 cup finely chopped fresh mint
1 teaspoon dried oregano
Salt
1 pound vermicelli pasta

In a medium skillet, melt butter, add garlic and sauté until golden. Remove sausage meat from casings, crumble and sauté until brown. Remove garlic. Add wine, mint and oregano. Salt to taste. Cover and simmer for 5 minutes. Turn off heat and let stand.

Cook vermicelli until al dente. Drain well and place in large serving bowl. Add sauce and mix well. Serve immediately in soup bowls.

Serves 4.

Winter Vegetable Sauce

6 tablespoons olive oil
1 dried red chili pepper (use less for a milder sauce)
2 cloves garlic, minced
1 can Italian plum tomatoes (28 ounces)
Salt to taste
1 teaspoon dried basil
3 bay leaves
2 cups broccoli flowerettes, steamed al dente
2 cups cauliflower flowerettes, steamed al dente
1/2 cup California dry sherry wine

In a large skillet, heat oil and sauté chili pepper with garlic until lightly golden. Squeeze or crush tomatoes by hand and add them with salt, basil and bay leaves to the skillet. Mix well, cover and cook for 20 minutes over moderate heat. Add vegetables and sherry. Cover and simmer for 5 minutes. Turn off flame, remove bay leaves and chili pepper and let stand while pasta cooks. Heat up quickly before serving.
Serves 6

Pesto For Pasta

When basil is abundant in the summer, make a year's supply to keep in your freezer. No need to wash blender between batches.

2 cups basil leaves without stems, washed and dried
1 tablespoon minced garlic (about 6 cloves)
1/2 cup good quality olive oil
3/4 cup grated Parmesan or Romano cheese (about 3 ounces)
2 tablespoons pine nuts

Place basil leaves, garlic, oil, cheese and pine nuts in blender and grate or chop until leaves are blended. Scrape down sides and purée until mixture is thoroughly blended. Scrape sides down again and check for any unblended garlic. Continue to blend until mixture is smooth. At this point the mixture will be bright green and look somewhat curdled.

If not using pesto immediately, place 1 tablespoon of mixture into an ice cube square. Cover tray with plastic wrap and freeze. When solid, unmold cubes and place in small baggie or wrap individually in foil. This recipe makes 8 or 9 cubes.

RED OR WHITE WINE WITH PASTA?

If your pasta sauce is abundantly flavored with garlic, herbs and tomato, try a hearty red wine such as Zinfandel or Petite Sirah. If your sauce is more delicate or you prefer white wine, serve a full-bodied white, either Chardonnay or Sauvignon Blanc.

One gallon finger handle jug

Half gallon jug before metric was mandatory. January 1, 1979.
(See page 69)

Shells and Zucchini

3 medium zucchini
1 carrot, coarsely chopped
1 yellow onion, coarsely chopped
3 tablespoons olive oil
1/2 teaspoon oregano
1 tablespoon fresh basil (or 1/2 teaspoon dried)
2 tablespoons marinara sauce
1 can chicken broth (14-1/2 ounces)
1/2 cup California dry white wine
1/2 cup grated Parmesan cheese
1 cup small macaroni shells

Partially peel washed zucchini, leaving some green skin for color. Remove a thick slice from each end and quarter zucchini lengthwise. Cut zucchini into 1/4-inch slices. Chop carrots and onions into small pieces.

In a large pan or Dutch oven, heat oil and sauté carrots with onions until onion is golden. Add zucchini, oregano, basil and marinara sauce. Mix well and stir for a few minutes. Add broth and wine. Cover and simmer for a few minutes. Bring to a boil, stirring in cheese. Simmer for 15 minutes. Season to taste.

Cook macaroni shells until al dente. Drain and add to other ingredients. Stir well, and simmer for 5 minutes. Serve in soup bowls with additional cheese sprinkled over individual servings.
Serves 6

Brothers, Tony and Vince, circa 1936.

Garlic Pasta Sauce

This sauce always disappears first at a pasta party. Serve it in a small gravy boat, explaining to guests that a little goes a long way.

1/2 cup garlic, peeled and finely minced
1/2 cup butter
1/2 cup olive oil
1 cup parsley, finely minced

Cook garlic in butter and oil over medium heat until soft but not browned. Lower heat and simmer for at least one hour. Add parsley and cook, stirring for 1 to 2 minutes until limp. Serve immediately.

Seafood

Family Friends

We remember the Busalacchis, for it was Peter who saved the Indelicato property from foreclosure.

Times were so tough during the Depression that Dad couldn't even make the interest payments on the land. It looked as if there was no way out. When the Busalacchis learned of our trouble, they went to a friend at the Bank of Stockton and pleaded for an extension on the loan. Without that favor, there would be no winery here.

— Frank, Tony and Vince Indelicato

We met Gaspare in Lodi a long time ago where we all worked harvesting grapes. In 1921 we attended the double wedding of Caterina and her twin sister, Serafina, to Gaspare Indelicato and Sebastiano Luppino.

When we got married in 1927, Caterina and Gaspare were at the wedding. The painting of a sunset over a lake—maybe it's in Italy—that hangs over our dining room buffet was the Indelicato gift to us. It's been there since we moved into this house after our honeymoon.

We were friends for a long time. We'd drive out to visit them on Sundays. In summer Gaspare would send us to the watermelon patch where we'd eat as much as we wanted. When it was time to go home, he'd load us up with whatever he had—a box of grapes or a sack of vegetables.

We remember Gaspare coming into Stockton on Wednesdays and Fridays in his old truck to sell wine. He'd come by our fish market to deliver wine. We usually sent fish home for his family. He'd take plenty of scraps, for Caterina made a fine fish head soup.

They were poor people. They had nothing materially, but they were happy on the land and always shared with others. If Gaspare were here today he wouldn't believe how the winery has grown and how well his children have done. He'd be proud.

—Mary and Frank Busalacchi

Busalacchi Fish Market. Stockton, CA.

Delta Catfish With Garlic

"We've been cooking our fish like this for years. It's simple and so good," says Frank Busalacchi, who met Gaspare Indelicato in the early 1920's when they both worked in Lodi-area vineyards. "I wish I could say we used wine to cook it, but we don't. We save all the wine to drink with the fish."

1 catfish (about 8 ounces) skinned, cleaned with head and tail removed*
2 tablespoons olive oil
3 cloves garlic, minced (about 1 tablespoon)
2 tablespoons parsley, minced
1 tablespoon fresh basil, minced or 1/2 teaspoon dried basil
1/2 cup hot water
Salt and pepper to taste
2 tablespoons Romano or Parmesan cheese, grated

Sauté garlic in olive oil until limp and lightly golden. Add fish and sauté until browned, turning once. Another tablespoon of oil may be needed.

Add parsley, basil and hot water. Season to taste. Cover and reduce heat. Simmer for 10 to 15 minutes, or until fish is cooked through. Check occasionally to be sure there is still liquid in the pan.

Remove fish to heated serving plate. Stir remaining liquid with garlic/herb mixture and pour over fish. Sprinkle cheese on top. Makes a single portion.

*Rock cod or sole fillets may be substituted.

Wine Suggestion: California Petite Sirah or Zinfandel.

Filleting fish, circa 1929.

Sumptuous Snapper

Prepared at the last minute, this sauce goes well on chicken and ham, too.

4 thin red snapper fillets (3 to 4 ounces each)
Flour for dredging
1 tablespoon olive oil
1 tablespoon butter
1 tablespoon country style Dijon mustard (with seeds)
2 tablespoons California dry white wine
1/2 cup heavy cream
1 tablespoon butter
Salt and pepper to taste

Melt oil and butter in skillet. Lightly dredge fish fillets in flour. Sauté over medium heat about 3 minutes on each side, turning only once. Remove to warm serving plate and keep hot.

In smaller pan, blend mustard and wine over medium-high heat for 1 minute. Reduce heat, add cream and whisk while reducing sauce by one-fourth. Remove pan from heat, whisk in butter, season to taste and pour over hot fish. Serve at once.

Serves 2 to 4.

Wine Suggestion: California Chardonnay.

Baked Perch

Cheese and bread crumbs bubble together atop perch fillets.

1 tablespoon butter
2 pounds perch fillets
4 shallots, minced
3 tablespoons butter
Salt and pepper to taste
1 cup California dry white wine, heated
1/2 cup fresh bread crumbs
3 / 4 cup Swiss cheese, grated

Preheat oven to 400°. Place fillets in buttered baking dish. Add shallots and dot with remaining butter. Season with salt and pepper. Cover fish with heated wine and bake for 15 minutes or until done. Remove dish from oven and sprinkle with crumbs and grated cheese. Brown under broiler until lightly browned and bubbly. Serve immediately. Serves 6.

Wine Suggestion: California Sauvignon Blanc or Zinfandel.

Grilled Whole Trout

Sea and orchard come together with a light touch of orange.

1 whole trout per person
Lemon wedges for garnish

MARINADE:

1 cup California Sauvignon Blanc wine
1 tablespoon grated orange rind
8 bay leaves, broken
6 peppercorns, crushed
1/4 cup fresh orange juice
2 tablespoons olive oil

Marinate fish in glass dish for 1 hour. Grill over hot mesquite charcoal until flesh is flaky, turning fish once. Serve immediately with lemon wedges.

Wine Suggestion: California Viognier.

Spirited Sole

A soul-satisfying fish dish simmered in wine.

Butter for greasing dish
1 pound sole fillets (or other firm white fish)
2 green onions, chopped, including greens
1/2 cup California Sauvignon Blanc wine
Water as needed (or more wine)
1 tablespoon butter
1 tablespoon flour
Salt and pepper to taste
Cayenne pepper to taste
1/4 cup ripe olives, thinly sliced
Parsley for garnish

Put fillets in greased skillet or shallow baking dish. Sprinkle onions on top and in between fish pieces. Pour wine over fillets then simmer 10 to 15 minutes, covered. When fish is flaky, remove fillets to heated platter and reserve liquid.

Melt butter and blend in flour, making a smooth paste. Add strained fish poaching liquid, salt, pepper and desired amount of cayenne, stirring until a medium-thick sauce is achieved. Add olives and parsley and pour over fish. Makes 3 or 4 servings.

Wine Suggestion: California Merlot.

In 1944 Frances got engaged to Joe Sciabica, whose mother came from the same town in Sicily as Dad. Everyone still talks about the engagement party that hot summer day. Joe butchered an 800-pound steer and cut it into steaks. Dad made a special grill in the backyard and 150 family and friends ate meat like they hadn't seen it for fifteen years. We had salads and fruit and lots of wine and some of the guests who had come from a distance stayed for a visit.

— Frank Indelicato

In 1944 Frances became engaged to
Joe Sciabica.

Scallop Sauté

The winery grew slowly but steadily. By 1940 a gallon of wine had gone from 50 to 95 cents. Because wine production was limited during the war years, the winery sold all it made and by 1944 the price soared to $1.90 a gallon. Those profitable times allowed Mom and Dad to build the family brick house and to make their only trip back to Italy.

In the early fifties we three brothers joined the business. In 1955 production reached 74,107 gallons—a long way from the 3,451 gallons of twenty years earlier. When Dad passed away in 1962, we were still a small, struggling winery.

At that time Tony was the winemaker, Vince was selling on the road and I was cellar manager. Dorothy was hired at 30 dollars a month as the first office clerk. She worked in the unheated office in front of the fermenters and complained of light-headedness from the fumes. It was a big occasion when we finally bought her a used Monroe calculator.

— Frank Indelicato

When the rice is almost ready, start the scallops. They'll be done in just five minutes.

1/4 cup olive oil
2 tablespoons coarsely minced shallots
Flour for dusting scallops
1 pound bay scallops
3/4 cup California Chardonnay wine
Steamed rice
Minced parsley for garnish
Lemon wedges for garnish

Heat oil in large, shallow skillet. Add shallots and sauté until limp. Lightly flour scallops and add to skillet. Sauté over high heat, shaking pan for 3 minutes. (Shaking pan but not stirring.)

Add wine and simmer for 2 minutes. Serve over rice. Garnish liberally with parsley and accompany with lemon wedges.
Serves 4.

Wine Suggestion: California Chardonnay.

Variation: Sauté 1/4 cup thinly sliced mushrooms with scallops.

Washing jugs on Saturdays and Sundays to prepare for bottling the next day.
Gaspare and Sebastiano on the right.

Homer's Marinated Crab

Homer Hamilton, a friend of the family, cooked for many fundraisers in our small community. His marinated crab recipe is our favorite.

2 cups olive oil
2 cups tomato sauce
½ cup lemon juice
2 cups red wine vinegar
Salt and pepper to taste
5 teaspoons garlic powder
8 whole dungeness crabs

Mix first six items and allow to marinate in the refrigerator for a couple of hours.

Clean and crack the crab legs, body, etc. and add to the marinade.

Marinate cracked crab for six to nine hours.turning every hour or so.

Serve Homer's Marinaded Crab with pasta, green salad, fresh French bread and your favorite wine. (Vince likes Cabernet and I like Chardonnay.)

Dad always said he planted a garden but raised kids. He believed in the value of work, so we all did chores every day around the farm. If we ran out of things to do, there were always bottles to wash, for in those days bottles were returnable.

We had been told since we were three-feet high that we'd go to college. Dad often told the story of how he asked his own father in Sicily if he could go to school.

"You want to be a lawyer?" the father asked his son. "No," Gaspare admitted. "I don't want to be a lawyer. I just want to learn." But his father was unconvinced and when Dad left Italy for America, he had only one year of schooling.

— Frank Indelicato

Costly Changes for Our Industry

In 1976 we were advised by Alcohol, Tobacco and Firearms of the upcoming metric system changes due on all of our tanks, barrels, and glassware. Prior to 1976 all our containers were measured in gallons.

It became mandatory on January 1,1979 for the wine industry and one year later for the distilled spirits industry to change all bottles to the metric system.
(See chart on your left.)

DEPARTMENT OF THE TREASURY
BUREAU OF ALCOHOL, TOBACCO AND FIREARMS
WINE

(handwritten: 4 oz = 10.57, 6 oz = 15.85)

BOTTLE SIZE	EQUIVALENT FLUID OUNCES	BOTTLES PER CASE	LITERS PER CASE	U.S. GALLONS PER CASE	CORRESPONDS TO
3 liters	101 Fl. Oz.	4	12.00	3.17004	4/5 Gallon
1.5 liters	50.7 Fl. Oz.	6	9.00	2.37753	2/5 Gallon
1 liter	33.8 Fl. Oz.	12	12.00	3.17004	1 Quart
750 milliliters	25.4 Fl. Oz.	12	9.00	2.37753	4/5 Quart
375 milliliters	12.7 Fl. Oz.	24	9.00	2.37753	4/5 Pint
187 milliliters	6.3 Fl. Oz.	48	8.976	2.37119	2/5 Pint
100 milliliters	3.4 Fl. Oz.	60	6.00	1.58502	2, 3, & 4 Oz.

(handwritten annotations: 4 liter; liters - 12L; 10 liters Pouch; 16.00; 4.22672; 2.6417; 1.183395; 18 liter; 4.75506; Gal ÷ .26417 = Liter; 187 - 24's; 18)

Official Conversion Factor: 1 Liter = 0.26417 U.S. Gallon.
Mandatory date for conversion: January 1, 1979.

ATF F 5100.10 (9-76)

DEPARTMENT OF THE TREASURY
BUREAU OF ALCOHOL, TOBACCO AND FIREARMS
DISTILLED SPIRITS

BOTTLE SIZE	EQUIVALENT FLUID OUNCES	BOTTLES PER CASE	LITERS PER CASE	U.S. GALLONS PER CASE	CORRESPONDS TO
1.75 liters	59.2 Fl. Oz.	6	10.50	2.773806	1/2 Gallon
1.00 liter	33.8 Fl. Oz.	12	12.00	3.170064	1 Quart
750 milliliters	25.4 Fl. Oz.	12	9.00	2.377548	4/5 Quart
500 milliliters	16.9 Fl. Oz.	24	12.00	3.170064	1 Pint
200 milliliters	6.8 Fl. Oz.	48	9.60	2.536051	1/2 Pint
50 milliliters	1.7 Fl. Oz.	120	6.00	1.585032	1, 1.6, & 2 Oz.

Official Conversion Factor: 1 Liter = 0.264172 U.S. Gallon.
Mandatory date for conversion: January 1, 1980.

ATF F 5100.10 (9-76)

Three Fish Sauces

I. MUSTARD SAUCE

1 tablespoon butter
1 tablespoon flour
1 cup bottled clam juice
1/4 teaspoon lemon juice
1 tablespoon green onion or shallot very finely minced
1 teaspoon prepared brown mustard
1-1/2 tablespoons California dry white wine

Melt butter. Blend in flour and cook over low heat for 2 minutes. Gradually add clam juice, stirring until slightly thickened. Combine lemon juice, onion, mustard and wine. Simmer 10 minutes over very low heat. Makes 3/4 cup sauce.
Enough for 2 servings.

II. SWEET AND SOUR SAUCE

1 can pineapple chunks (15-1/2 ounces), reserve liquid
1-1/2 tablespoons cornstarch
1/2 cup pineapple juice reserved from can
1/2 tablespoon soy sauce
1/4 cup white wine vinegar
1/4 cup California dry white wine
1/4 cup minced celery
1/4 cup minced scallions

Mix cornstarch with reserved pineapple juice until smooth. Add soy sauce, white vinegar and wine then cook over low heat until sauce thickens, stirring constantly. Add celery and scallions and simmer for a few minutes, continuing to stir. Add pineapple chunks and simmer over very low heat for about 5 minutes. Pour over cooked fish. Also delicious on pork and chicken. Makes 1-1/2 cups.

III PAPRIKA SAUCE

1 shallot or green onion, finely minced
1 large clove garlic, finely minced
2 tablespoons butter
2 tablespoons flour
1 cup bottled clam juice or fish stock
1/4 cup California dry white wine
1 tablespoon sour cream
1 tablespoon lemon juice
2 teaspoons paprika

Sauté minced shallot or green onion and garlic in butter until tender. Stir in flour and cook over low heat for 2 minutes. Gradually add clam juice or fish stock and wine, stirring constantly until well blended and thickened. Add sour cream, lemon juice and paprika. Makes 1 cup.

First company party was to a 1960 San Francisco baseball game.
Bottom row: Terry Larranaga, Mary, Alice, Ida and George Koyl.
Top row: Tony, Vince, Frank, Joe Larranaga
Photographed by Dorothy

Dorothy's Cioppino

1 cup extra virgin olive oil
2 large onions, minced
½ bunch fresh parsley, minced
4 large cloves garlic, minced
2 can chopped tomatoes (28 ounces)
2 cans tomato sauce (15 ounces)
2-3 bay leaves
½ teaspoon dried basil
2 tablespoons chili powder
1 small can anchovies
2 pounds codfish chopped into 3" pieces
4 cooked, cleaned cracked crabs in shell (about 2 pounds each)
2 pounds (26-30 per pound) shrimp
2 pounds large scallops
2 pounds clams
2 cups dry white wine

In a large pot (16 quarts), lightly sauté onions in olive oil. After 2 minutes, add parsley, garlic, tomatoes and tomato sauce. Bring to a simmer, stirring often. Add anchovies and spices, bring back to a simmer and cook for 1 hour. Add cod; return to simmer, stirring often. This fish will thicken the sauce, simmer for about 2 hours.

Add crab, stirring it into the sauce, followed by the shrimp. (If sauce is too thick, add tomato juice). Return to simmer. Stir in scallops, clams. Add white wine and continue to simmer until clams open. Cioppino is ready to serve.

Serves 15 people. Goes well with rice or mashed potatoes. Serve with French bread.

Wine Suggestions: California Chardonnay or Merlot.

LUMACHE (Loo-mah-chay)

After snails were picked from the garden, Caterina washed them under the faucet and kept only the ones that could crawl off a slick surface.

DAY 1: For at least 2 weeks she kept the snails in a box and fed them only cornmeal, greens and fresh water.

DAY 15: She took away the greens for 48 hours, but continued to feed them cornmeal and fresh water.

DAY 17: For the next 48 hours she took away the cornmeal, but left fresh water for them to drink.

DAY 19: When their systems were flushed out from this diet, she dropped the snails into a pot of boiling water and cooked them for 10 minutes. Then she removed them from the hot water, let them cool, and removed the meat from the shells.

The cooked snails were either fixed cioppino-style in tomato sauce or dipped in Joe Sciabica's Garlic Sauce (See page 72).

Nanna liked snails. Because I was a small child, I remember her as a big lady, even though she was only five feet tall. She was a gentle lady. I remember the days when she'd hand me an empty coffee can and I'd head into the garden to find snails. When I had it filled, she'd give me candy. When she cooked the snails, I ate some, but I remember thinking they were pretty chewy.
—Robert Indelicato

I remember how the snails got into the family garden in the first place: When Gaspare made trips to San Francisco, he'd stop by the cemeteries and gather snails to bring home. They're prolific creatures and soon we had all we could eat.
—Joe Sciabica

Cod Navarro Style

Bacalao Navarro

Joe Larranaga, a Delicato employee for 25 years, grew up in a home filled with the rich smells of Basque cooking. Joe's parents came from the provinces bordering France. Joe and his wife, Theresa, cooked traditional Basque family recipes as well as recipes gathered during a visit to the ancestral land. I recently learned that Joe had received several medals as a result of his participation in the invasion of Normandy during World War II. He was only 19 at the time.

— Dorothy Indelicato

2 pounds salt cod
2 medium onions, chopped
2 cloves garlic, minced
1 can minced pimentos (4 ounces, drained)
1/4 cup olive oil
1 can tomato sauce (8 ounces)
1/2 cup minced parsley
1/2 cup California dry white wine

Wash the cod, changing water 3 or 4 times to remove the salt. Place the cod in a pot, cover in water and soak it overnight. Drain water, cut fish into 2-inch pieces then cover again in cold water. Bring to a boil then remove fish and set aside.

Sauté onions, garlic and pimentos in olive oil. When vegetables are tender, return the cod to the pot then stir in tomato sauce, parsley and wine. Cover and simmer for 30 minutes or until fish flakes easily.

Serves 4 to 6.

Family driveway in 1948.
Note: One house with two garages.

Joe's Garlic Sauce

1 head garlic, peeled (8 to 10 cloves)
1/2 teaspoon salt
4 to 5 sprigs parsley or sweet basil
1 teaspoon olive oil
1/2 to 3/4 cup cold water

Mash garlic in mortar or grind lightly in blender or food processor. Add salt, parsley or basil, and olive oil. Mix well. Add water for desired consistency.

Poultry

It is an old tradition to celebrate the grape harvest by crushing grapes the way it was done many, many years ago. Delicato thought that it might be fun to show the younger generation the technique during a charity fundraiser. Delicato conducted this fundraiser for 19 years until the event grew too large to continue.

During the Stomp, each stomper/pair of stompers was given 90 seconds to "crush" as much juice as they could from 25 pounds of grapes that had been dumped into a large half barrel. The stompers wore old tennis shoes for safety and to enhance their effectiveness. The juice yielded was then measured and the winners of each category were recognized at the awards ceremony at the end of the event.

The juice was later put into the pomace pile and made into compost, which would restore nutrients to the vineyard.

Grape stompers in competition at one of the annual fundraisers.

Grape stomp trophies.

Chicken Cacciatori

This family recipe is often served over rice or spaghetti.

1 chicken (3 to 4 pounds), cut up
4 tablespoons olive oil
Salt and pepper to taste
1 tablespoon dried, minced garlic
2 tablespoons minced parsley
2 teaspoons Italian seasoning
1/2 cup thinly sliced mushrooms
4 cans tomato sauce (8 ounces each)
1 cup water
1 cup California Pinot Grigio

Brown chicken pieces in oil until golden brown. Season with salt and pepper as chicken browns. Add garlic, parsley, Italian seasoning, mushrooms, tomato sauce, water and wine. Cover and simmer for 35 minutes. Remove cover and simmer an additional 10 minutes. Serves 4 to 5.

Wine Suggestion: California Pinot Grigio.

Chardonnay Chicken

4 large cloves fresh garlic, peeled
3 tablespoons butter
3 tablespoons olive oil
1 chicken (3 pounds), cut up
Salt and pepper to taste
2 cups California Chardonnay
1 can whole peeled tomatoes (28 ounces), cut into quarters

Sauté garlic in butter and oil in large pan. Brown chicken. Season with salt and pepper. Simmer until tender. Remove chicken from pan and keep warm. Scrape bits of chicken from pan while stirring in wine. Reduce sauce by half over high heat. Add tomatoes, stir well and cook over moderate heat for about 10 minutes. Return chicken to pan, spooning sauce over chicken. Heat through and serve chicken in sauce. Serves 4.

Wine Suggestion: California Chardonnay.

Classic Chicken In Wine

1/4 pound diced bacon
1 tablespoon butter
1 chicken (3 pounds), cut up
3 tablespoons brandy, warmed
1 yellow onion, chopped
1 tablespoon flour
2 tablespoons tomato paste
3 cups California Cabernet Sauvignon
2 large garlic cloves
1 large bay leaf
2 tablespoons minced parsley
1/4 teaspoon thyme
Salt and pepper to taste
1/2 pound fresh mushrooms
1 tablespoon butter

Sauté bacon until crisp. Remove bacon. Sauté chicken in bacon grease until nicely browned. Pour in warmed brandy. Ignite, shaking pan until flames subside. Remove chicken and keep warm.

In the same pan, sauté onion with bacon drippings until translucent. Stir in flour and cook for 1 minute. Blend in tomato paste, wine, garlic and herbs. Season with salt and pepper. Bring to a boil, then lower heat and add chicken and bacon. Simmer for 1 hour, occasionally turning pieces in sauce.

When chicken is done, remove to warmed platter. Increase heat and reduce sauce to about 3 cups.

Sauté mushrooms in 1 tablespoon butter until limp. Set aside. Return chicken to sauce and add mushrooms. Heat through. Serves 4.

Wine Suggestion: California Cabernet Sauvignon or Zinfandel.

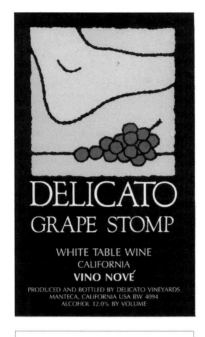

DELICATO
GRAPE STOMP
WHITE TABLE WINE
CALIFORNIA
VINO NOVÉ
PRODUCED AND BOTTLED BY DELICATO VINEYARDS
MANTECA, CALIFORNIA USA BW 4094
ALCOHOL 12.0% BY VOLUME

DELICATO CHARITY GRAPE STOMP 1991

It is an old tradition to celebrate the grape crush by crushing grapes the way they were crushed many, many years ago. Delicato Vineyards wishes to carry on this tradition. What better way than to have fun, carry on tradition and help our community all at the same time with a charity fund raiser.

What happens during the Stomp? Each stomper/pair of stompers is given 90 seconds to "crush" as much juice as they can from a 25 pound lug of grapes which has been dumped into a large half barrel. The stompers wear old tennis shoes for safety and to enhance their effectiveness. The juice yielded is then measured and the winners of each category recognized at the awards ceremony at the end of the event.

Stomp record holders as of September 1990 are:

Category	Name of Record Holder	City	Age Group	Ounces	Year
Pee Wee	Brendon Bombaci	Manteca	5 yrs. or younger	19.2	1987
Junior	Jarrod Schwartz	Manteca	6-12 yrs. of age	76.0	1990
Adult-Female	Tracy Zak	Union City	13-60 yrs. of age	88.0	1987
Adult-Male	Todd Berg	Clements	13-60 yrs. of age	137.5	1988
Seniors	Alice McGhan	Manteca	Over 60 yrs. of age	100.2	1987
Junior Doubles	Justin & Zac Wilkins	Fremont	2 contestants per barrel, 0-12 yrs.	78.0	1989
Mixed Doubles	Richard Burton & Debbie Buriani	Modesto Modesto	1 female and 1 male per barrel	121.5	1987
Doubles	Clay & Michael Baxter	Manteca	2 contestants per barrel-same gender	121.5	1990
Corporate Sponsors	Able 2 Staff	Manteca	4 contestants in 2 barrels (averaged)	168.0	1990

This special bottling, to commemorate the ninth year of the Delicato Charity Grape Stomp, is called VINO NOVE which means "Wine of the Ninth". Look forward to "Wine of the Tenth".

Serve chilled — 45 to 50° F. . . . Enjoy!

DELICATO
GRAPE STOMP
CALIFORNIA
TABLE WINE
VINO UNDICI
MADE AND BOTTLED BY DELICATO VINEYARDS
MANTECA, CALIFORNIA USA BW 4094
ALCOHOL 11.0% BY VOLUME

1993
DELICATO CHARITY GRAPE STOMP

It is an old tradition to celebrate the grape crush by crushing grapes the way they were crushed many, many years ago. Delicato Vineyards wishes to carry on this tradition. What better way than to have fun, carry on tradition and help our community all at the same time with a charity fund raiser.

What happens during the Stomp? Each stomper/pair of stompers is given 90 seconds to "crush" as much juice as they can from a 25 pound lug of grapes which has been dumped into a large half barrel. The stompers wear old tennis shoes for safety and to enhance their effectiveness. The juice yielded is then measured and the winners of each category recognized at the awards ceremony at the end of the event.

Stomp record holders as of September 1992 are:

Category	Name of Record Holder	City	Age Group	Ounces	Year
Pee Wee	Brendon Bombaci	Manteca	5 yrs. or younger	19.2	1987
Junior	Jarrod Schwartz	Manteca	6-12 yrs. of age	76.0	1990
Adult-Female	Tracy Zak	Union City	13-60 yrs. of age	88.0	1987
Adult-Male	Todd Berg	Clements	13-60 yrs. of age	137.5	1988
Seniors	Alice McGhan	Manteca	Over 60 yrs. of age	100.2	1987
Junior Doubles	Scott Allen & Joey Smith	Stockton	2 contestants per barrel, 0-12 yrs.	84.0	1992
Mixed Doubles	Richard Burton & Debbie Buriani	Modesto Modesto	1 female and 1 male per barrel	121.5	1987
Doubles	Gary & Larry Burlingame	Manteca	2 contestants per barrel-same gender	181.2	1992
Corporate Sponsors	Able 2 Staff	Manteca	4 contestants in 2 barrels (averaged)	168.0	1990

This special bottling, to commemorate the eleventh year of the Delicato Charity Grape Stomp, is called VINO UNDICI (pronounced OON' duh che) which means "Wine of the Eleventh". Look forward to "VINO DODICI", Wine of the Twelfth.

Serve at temperature — 45 to 50° F. . . . Enjoy!

In Sicily, Dad's grandfather and father made wine once a year from grapes they grew on a small plot of land near the house. When Dad came to this country, he did the same thing.

When Dad started his winery, he no longer needed to make family wine, but he remembered others who did and provided them with bulk grape juice. Today, we still supply amateur winemakers with high-quality juice.

Each autumn during the crush, our parking lot is jammed with pickups and trailers loaded with empty wine barrels. Many of these home wine producers drive hundreds of miles, from as far away as Nevada, Idaho and Arizona. Some come every year, getting here early to visit with old friends, share winemaking secrets, and enjoy a picnic breakfast while they wait for the winery to open.

It's not the idea of saving money that brings people here. It's the excitement of being in touch with the land, the same excitement that comes from planting a garden or preparing a good meal. People like being part of a tradition that goes back to the founding of our winery and recalling the customs of the Old Country.

—Frank Indelicato

Home winemaker and grape juice buyer, 1982.

Coq Au Vin

Coq au Vin (coke-oh-van) is a French country dish in which the wine is every bit as important as the chicken. Together they simmer with onions and herbs, then are joined by mushrooms at the finish to create a hearty main dish.

The City of Chanturge in France's Auvergne region claims it was the first to cook Coq au Vin, although the Burgundy area says it invented the popular dish. Today every province of France creates its own version, using wine from the area.

Traditional recipes used robust red wines, but soon white wines—even champagnes—became part of the recipe. Today, Coq au Vin recipes include almost every red and white wine. Julia Child urged her readers to experiment with different wines, renaming the dish "Coq au Riesling" or "Coq au Whatever," after the wine used. *The Joy of Cooking* recommends a variation using sherry.

I suggest using Delicato red wines: Cabernet Sauvignon or Merlot; and Delicato white wines: Chardonnay or Sauvignon Blanc. Try a different wine each time you prepare these recipes. You'll notice slight differences and will soon discover your favorite combination.   -----Dorothy Indelicato

Mustard Chicken

2 tablespoons butter
2 tablespoons olive oil
1 chicken (approx. 3 pounds), cut up
2 cups California white wine
1/4 teaspoon dried tarragon
Pinch thyme
1 large bay leaf
Salt and pepper to taste
2 egg yolks
2 tablespoons country style Dijon mustard (with seeds)
2 tablespoons sour cream
Pinch cayenne pepper

Melt butter in olive oil. Add chicken and cook until well browned. Add wine, tarragon, thyme, bay leaf, salt and pepper. Bring to boil. Cover and simmer 45 minutes. Remove chicken to heated serving dish and keep warm.

Discard bay leaf. Blend sauce with egg yolks. Add mustard, sour cream and cayenne. Heat, stirring continually. Do not allow to boil. Pour over chicken. Serves 4 to 6.

Serve with plenty of rice to soak up the wonderful sauce. Steamed carrots and zucchini slices are colorful and tasty additions. End with Peach Topping (page 129) over cinnamon ice cream.

Wine Suggestion: California Petite Sirah.

Roast Chicken

8 cups water
1 whole chicken (about 3 pounds)
1/2 lemon
2 garlic cloves, crushed
Paprika
Sesame sauce (page 78)

Boil water. Preheat oven to 475°.

Rinse chicken in cold water and pat dry. Rub skin and cavity of chicken with lemon half and garlic cloves. Place both in cavity. Put chicken in shallow roaster, breast side down. Sprinkle generously with paprika. Pour boiling water into roaster (but not on chicken) to a depth of one inch. Place on top rack of oven.

Roast chicken for 15 minutes at 475°. Turn chicken and lower heat to 350°. Cook for an additional 40 to 45 minutes. Place the roaster in the lower pan which contains an ample supply of water. Keep at least 1/2 inch of water in roaster.
Serves 4.

Wine Suggestion: California Chardonnay.

Home winemakers at Delicato, 1982.

Rowdy Chicken

1 chicken (about 3 pounds), cut up
1 tablespoon dried rosemary
2 tablespoons olive oil
4 cloves garlic, minced
1/3 of 2-ounce can anchovies in oil
3/4 cup California dry white wine, divided
3/4 cup heavy cream

Dredge chicken pieces in rosemary. Heat oil and sauté garlic until it begins to brown. Add chicken and fry until brown, turning often.

Mince anchovy fillets and mix with 1/2 cup wine. Pour over chicken and simmer uncovered 30 to 40 minutes. Baste occasionally with sauce, adding additional 1/4 cup of wine if needed.

Remove chicken to heated serving plate. To create sauce, add 3/4 cup heavy cream to skillet, stirring to loosen particles at bottom. Serves 4 to 6.

Wine Suggestion: California Petite Sirah.

Chicken In Moscato

Offers a touch of sweetness and the crunch of nuts.

1/2 cup golden raisins
1 1/4 cup California Moscato wine
1 chicken (3 pounds), cut up
1 tablespoon butter
1 tablespoon oil
1 medium onion, minced
6 whole cloves
1 bay leaf
1/2 teaspoon cumin
1 cup chicken stock
1/2 cup heavy cream
2 egg yolks
Salt and pepper to taste
1/2 cup almonds, slivered, blanched and salted

Plump raisins in 1/4 cup wine. Brown chicken in butter and oil. Add onion, sautéing until translucent. Add cloves, bay leaf, cumin and stock. Cover and simmer gently, adding raisins and wine. Remove chicken to a heated serving platter and keep warm while preparing the sauce.

Mix cream, egg yolks and 1 cup of wine. Stir in a small amount of hot chicken sauce and pour all into chicken pot. Stir gently for several minutes until slightly thickened. Do not allow sauce to boil.
Serves 4.

Accompany with plenty of white or brown rice and steamed, chopped spinach.

Wine Suggestion: California Riesling.

Letter from a satisfied customer.

Sesame Sauce

1 cup California Sauvignon Blanc wine
1/2 cup olive oil
1/4 teaspoon red pepper flakes (optional)
Salt to taste
2 garlic cloves, finely minced
1/3 cup sesame seeds, lightly toasted

Whisk wine, oil, pepper flakes, salt and garlic together. Add sesame seeds. Serve over fish, chicken or meat. Makes about 2 cups.

Chicken With Nutmeg

1 chicken (3 pounds), cut up
3 tablespoons olive oil
2 medium onions, thinly sliced
3 large garlic cloves, minced
1 whole nutmeg, grated or 3 teaspoons ground nutmeg
1 teaspoon thyme
2 tablespoons fresh parsley or cilantro, minced
1 cup chicken broth, heated
2/3 cup California dry sherry wine

In a large pot, brown chicken pieces in olive oil. Remove chicken and set aside. Add onions and garlic to drippings and cook until soft and golden.

Combine nutmeg, salt, thyme and parsley (or cilantro) with onions, stirring well. Return chicken to pot. Add broth and half of sherry and bring to a boil. Reduce heat, cover, and simmer for 1 hour. Stir in remaining sherry just before serving.
Serves 4 to 6.

Accompany with crunchy brown rice, steamed carrots and a simple dessert of vanilla ice cream with a splash of California Late Harvest Reisling wine.

Wine Suggestion: California red wine blend.

1st Tasting Room Sign, circa 1963.

Crunchy Brown Rice

3 cups chicken stock
1-1/2 cups uncooked long grain brown rice
1 teaspoon ground turmeric (optional)
1/3 cup dried currants
1/4 cup California dry sherry wine
2 tablespoons green onions, finely minced
1/3 cup pine nuts (or sunflower kernels)
3/4 teaspoon preserved ginger, minced
2 tablespoons butter

Cook rice according to package instructions, substituting chicken stock for water.

Remove from heat and stir in remaining ingredients. Let mixture absorb flavors a few minutes before serving.

Makes 4 to 6 servings.

Tasting Room directional billboard, circa 1993.

Chicken In Feta Sauce

3 tablespoons olive oil
1 chicken (3 pounds), cut up
1 tablespoon butter
3 medium yellow onions, thinly sliced
1 - 1/2 pounds peeled and chopped fresh tomatoes (or 28-ounce can)
1/2 cup California dry white wine
2 cloves garlic, minced
2 teaspoons dried rosemary
Freshly ground black pepper
Salt
1/2 pound Feta cheese

FACTS ABOUT FETA

Feta cheese (fet-ah) is commonplace in Greek and Balkan cooking. Soft, crumbly, and salty, this chalky white delicacy is made from ewe's or goat's milk and tastes a little like Roquefort. It is delicious on salads or vegetables. Spread it on unsalted crackers or buttered, crusty French bread for a quick, elegant hors d'oeuvres.

In a skillet heat 2 tablespoons olive oil. Halve chicken breast and brown 4 to 5 minutes on each side. Remove to platter. Sauté remaining chicken pieces for 15 minutes, turning occasionally. While chicken is browning, heat 1 tablespoon oil and 1 tablespoon butter in large skillet. Add sliced onions and cook over medium heat, stirring occasionally. Cook until translucent and slightly browned, about 15 minutes.

Add tomatoes (with juice if canned), wine, garlic and 1 teaspoon rosemary. Season with black pepper. Withhold any additional salt until end of cooking due to saltiness of cheese. Add chicken pieces, covering well with onions and sauce. Cover and simmer over medium-low heat for 20 minutes.

Crumble Feta cheese on top. Cover and cook 15 minutes. Additional wine or water may be needed during cooking. Taste and add salt, if needed. Ladle over ample helpings of white rice and sprinkle with additional crushed rosemary when serving. Serves 4 to 6.

Wine Suggestion: California light-bodied Zinfandel.

The original 1935 winery was housed in a former barn.
Note the tub used for washing bottles.

Chicken With Okra

Kotopaulo me Bamies

An often neglected vegetable in many parts of the U.S.A., okra takes center stage in this light chicken dish.

1 package frozen okra (10 ounces) or 1-1/2 pounds fresh okra, chopped
1 cup olive oil, divided
1 chicken (about 3 pounds), cut up
1 large onion, chopped (about 1 cup)
2 large cloves garlic, minced
1/2 cup California dry white wine

Place fresh or defrosted okra in small saucepan with 1/4 cup olive oil. Sauté over low heat until vegetable is lightly tinged with brown. Set aside. Or, place cut-up okra in ¼ cup olive oil and bake in 250° oven for 1 hour. Stir occasionally to ensure even browning.

Brown cut-up chicken in 1/2 cup olive oil. Reduce heat, add onion and garlic and cook until limp. Add wine. Simmer for 1 to 2 minutes. Add okra, reduce heat and continue simmering for 30 to 40 minutes. Check chicken occasionally and stir lightly. Add more wine near end of cooking if needed to create enough sauce for spooning over chicken and rice.

Serves 6.

A Greek salad and coconut cookies complete this Greek-inspired menu.

Wine Suggestion: California White Zinfandel.

Hint: To dissolve the gelatinous substance in okra, Greek cooks always soak the vegetable in vinegar before cooking. To prepare fresh okra, first wash vegetable and cut off stems. Place okra in bowl, adding 1/2 cup white or cider vinegar per pound of okra. Let stand one hour. Rinse thoroughly with cold water and drain. Proceed with recipe.

To prepare frozen okra, drop into boiling water. When pieces separate, drain well and place in bowl. Add 1/2 cup vinegar per pound of okra and let stand 15 minutes. Rinse thoroughly with cold water and drain.

Second home of the two families. First house was burned by children playing with matches.

Chicken In Zinfandel

First sales room of the winery.

1 chicken (3 pounds), cut up
4 tablespoons butter
1/2 pound mushrooms, sliced
3 slices bacon, chopped
Chicken giblets, minced
10 small onions, whole
3 cloves garlic
3 tablespoons brandy
2 cups California Zinfandel wine
Salt and pepper to taste
1 tablespoon flour

Remove chicken from port marinade and dry with paper towel. Strain and reserve marinade. Sauté chicken pieces in 2 tablespoons butter.

In a separate pan sauté mushrooms in 1 tablespoon butter until limp, then remove.

In the same pan fry bacon and chicken giblets together. When ready, remove to paper towel. Still using same pan, brown onions and cloves in remaining grease until lightly brown. Add onions, garlic, bacon and giblets to pan with chicken.

Add warm brandy and ignite, shaking pan until flames subside. Add Zinfandel plus 1 cup of reserved marinade. Cook 1 hour over moderate heat. Taste, then season with salt and pepper.

Remove chicken to serving platter and keep warm. Continue to cook until sauce is reduced to approximately 3 cups. Add mushrooms and heat through.

To thicken sauce, combine 1 tablespoon butter and 1 tablespoon flour in a bowl. Knead thoroughly, then shape into tiny balls. Drop a few at a time into the sauce, whisking briskly, until all are absorbed. Over low heat, stir sauce constantly for 1 minute. Do not boil. Simmer for an additional 5 minutes then pour over chicken.

Serves 4 to 6.

Wine Suggestion: California Zinfandel or Pinot Noir

PORT MARINADE:

2 cups California port wine
3 sprigs parsley
12 peppercorns
Bay leaf
1/8 teaspoon thyme

Whisk to combine all ingredients. Marinate chicken in a glass bowl for 24 to 48 hours in the refrigerator, turning occasionally.

Persian Chicken

Roasted chicken stuffed with bulgur, reminiscent of Middle Eastern flavors.

1 roasting chicken, about 3 1/2 pounds
Lemon wedge
Garlic clove
6 tablespoons melted butter, divided
1/2 cup minced white onion (or green onions with some tops)
1/2 cup bulgur (sometimes labeled pilaf)
1/2 teaspoon cinnamon
1 cup chicken broth
1/3 cup tomato sauce
1/4 cup finely chopped dried apricots
1/4 cup raisins
1/4 teaspoon salt
Black pepper to taste
1 teaspoon lemon juice
3 tablespoons honey
2 tablespoons California medium-dry sherry wine
3 tablespoons sesame seeds
Parsley sprigs, lemon slices, orange slices for garnish

Rub skin and cavity of chicken with lemon wedge and garlic clove.

In medium saucepan melt 3 tablespoons butter. Add onion, sautéing about 5 minutes. Add bulgur and stir constantly for 5 minutes. Add cinnamon, broth, tomato sauce, apricots, raisins, salt, pepper and lemon juice. Remove from heat. Let sit, covered, for 1 hour.

Preheat oven to 350°. In small saucepan heat honey, 3 tablespoons butter and sherry over low heat until butter melts. Stuff chicken with bulgur mixture and place in roasting pan. Roast in 350° oven for 75 minutes, brushing bird frequently with honey-butter-sherry mixture.

After 1 hour of baking, baste chicken for final time with mixture and drippings from pan. Scatter sesame seeds over chicken. Watch carefully for 15 minutes to avoid over-browning. Remove from oven, let stand 5 minutes before serving.

Place chicken on platter and surround with sprigs of parsley and lemon and orange slices. Carve at table, giving each guest a hearty helping of the steaming-hot dressing. Serves 4 to 6.

Wine Suggestion: California Pinot Grigio.

Entry to current tasting room.

BULGUR

When wheat kernels are boiled, dried, cracked, then sorted by size, the result is bulgar. This wheat product is sometimes referred to as "Middle Eastern pasta" for its versatility as a base for all sorts of dishes. Bulgur is most often made from durum wheat, but in fact almost any wheat, hard or soft, red or white, can be made into bulgur.

Because bulgur has been precooked and dried, it needs to be boiled for only about 10 minutes to be ready to eat, about the same time as dry pasta. This makes bulgur an extremely nutritious fast food for quick side dishes, pilaf or salads.

Health bonus: Bulgur has more fiber than quinoa, oats millet, buckwheat or corn. It's quick cooking time and mild flavor make it ideal for those new to whole grain cooking.

SAN BERNABE VINEYARDS

In 1842, the Cana de San Bernabe Mexican Land Grant was issued. This land has ancient sand dunes that are unique to the Monterey area.

In 1988 Delicato had the opportunity to purchase 13,148 acres of San Bernabe which was partially planted into several varieties of grapes. The vineyard, located 20 miles inland from Big Sur on the California coastline, covered some twenty-one square miles. San Bernabe was a viticulturist's dream come true. The property produced approximately one third of the grapes harvested in Monterey County, including much sought after Chardonnay, Zinfandel, Cabernet, Muscat Canelli, and Sauvignon Blanc. This large area of land has 21 micro climates, elevations and slopes with different wind exposures.

These challenges have allowed the winemakers and viticulturalists to develop very unique wines from this vineyard. In fact, in 2004 San Bernabe was granted its own AVA designation.*

San Bernabe Vineyards is also a Certified California Sustainable Winegrowing property -- One of the first vineyards in California to carry this designation.

American Viticultural Area (AVA)

An American Viticultural Area is a disignated wine grape-growing region in the United States distinguishable by geographic features, with boundaries defined by the Alcohol and Tobacco Tax and Trade Bureau (TTB) of the United States Department of the Treasury.

The TTB defines AVAs at the request of wineries and other petitioners. As of March 2015, there are 230 AVAs in the United States. Prior to the AVA system, wine appellations of origin in the United States were designated based on state or county boundaries.

Chicken With Spices

First fried crisp, then simmered in wine and spices, this chicken dish has a smooth texture and a sweet East Indian taste.

1 chicken (3 pounds), cut up
1/4 cup flour
1/2 cup olive oil
2 garlic cloves, minced
1 small onion, minced
1/8 teaspoon cinnamon
1/8 teaspoon cloves
2 cups California dry white wine
Salt to taste

Dust chicken lightly with flour. Heat olive oil in heavy skillet. Fry chicken until very brown and crisp. Remove chicken and pour off all but 2 tablespoons of oil.

Add garlic, onion, cinnamon and cloves and cook until onion is soft. Add wine and simmer for 10 minutes. Return chicken and simmer uncovered for about 15 minutes, until chicken is tender. Check for seasoning. Serves 4 to 6.

Delicious with wild rice, baked yams and perhaps a fruity dessert such as Apple Slices Baked In Red Wine (page 127).

Wine Suggestion: California Pinot Grigio.

Our San Bernabe Vineyards in Monterey County, was purchased in 1988.

Chicken On The Hot Side

Appetites will expand after the first bite, so prepare plenty. This recipe doubles easily for entertaining, keeps well in the refrigerator and improves with reheating.

2 tablespoons olive oil
3 pounds chicken pieces
1/2 cup shallots (or mild onions), minced
2 cloves garlic, halved
1 can whole tomatoes (28 ounces)
1 cup California dry white wine
1/2 teaspoon salt
1/4 teaspoon black pepper
1/4 teaspoon crushed red pepper
1/3 cup minced parsley

Heat oil in skillet. Brown chicken pieces until golden. Place in large ovenproof casserole.

In same skillet, sauté shallots and garlic for 3 minutes, adding more oil if necessary. Stir in tomatoes, wine, salt and pepper, red pepper and parsley. Simmer for 10 minutes and pour over chicken. Bake 1 hour at 350°. Serve over spinach fettuccine or egg noodles.
Serves 6.

Accompany with salad greens and a cooling fruit dessert such as Zabaglione (page127) drizzled over fresh fruit.

Wine Suggestions: California Zinfandel or Cabernet Sauvignon.

Our entire family still remembers one exciting Sunday in 1968 when the glass-lined tanks arrived from Texas at the Turner Station rail siding, just down the road from the winery. Until this time, all our wine was aged indoors in wooden tanks.

The six used tanks were unloaded from the railroad flat cars with a crane, hauled to the winery a half mile away, and placed on concrete foundations outside in the production area.

We were all there taking movies of the whole event. When the tanks were safely in place, we sat down for a big family meal and celebrated our new winemaking capacity—403,000 gallons—three times what we had been able to produce the year before.

— Dorothy Indelicato

Vince, Robert, and Marie meet the train carrying glass-lined tanks from Texas, 1968.

Italian Stuffed Turkey

SICLIAN STUFFED TURKEY -- ***Dorothy's Recipe***

FAMILY TURKEY

In America, turkey is traditionally served on Thanksgiving or Christmas, but our family had it on all special occasions, including Easter.

Mom fixed it the way she learned in the old country. When she added the potatoes, carrots and onions to the juice near the end of the cooking, we knew it was almost time to eat.

My sister Frances, or Francy as we call her, still prepares it the way she remembers Mom cooking it. We include all three recipes in the book for you. My wife, sister, and sister-in-law each have their own special way of cooking the dressing. All are delicious!

We have never served any one wine with the turkey dinner, but instead put out a selection of wines and let everyone drink his favorite.

–Vincent Indelicato

20-pound turkey
½ cup California dry red wine
1 cup California dry white wine
6 garlic cloves
Salt and pepper to taste
4 celery ribs, chopped
1 medium-sized onion, chopped
4 potatoes, peeled and quartered

DRESSING:

2 pounds ground beef
4 eggs
2 cups rice, steamed with salt, butter and parsley
1 large onion, coarsely chopped
Salt and pepper to taste
4 tablespoons fresh minced garlic
1 cup fresh parsley
2 cups California Zinfandel wine
1 cup grated Romano cheese

In large bowl combine beef, eggs, cooked steamed rice, onion, salt, pepper, garlic, parsley, red wine and cheese. Mix well. Stuff turkey with dressing. Place turkey in covered roaster and pour white wine over bird. Sprinkle with garlic salt and pepper to taste.

Put the roaster in unheated 500° oven for 20 minutes. Turn down heat to 400° and roast for 4 hours without removing the lid. Check turkey, opening lid away from you to avoid the steam which has generated during cooking.

Add celery, onions and potatoes and cook covered for an additional 30 minutes.

Wine Suggestion: California Chardonnay

Building concrete fermenters, 1953.

SOUTH ITALIAN STUFFED TURKEY   ----   *Francy's Recipe*

20-pound turkey
3 pounds ground beef
1 onion, chopped
3/4 cup cooked rice, cooled
4 tablespoons garlic, minced
1 teaspoon olive oil
Parsley to taste, minced
1 cup Romano cheese, grated
1 egg
Salt and pepper to taste
4 potatoes peeled and quartered
4 carrots, peeled and quartered
4 onions, quartered

DRESSING:

Combine ground beef, onion, rice, garlic, parsley, cheese, and egg. Mix well. Stuff turkey and close tightly with skewers or thread. Rub bird with olive oil, salt and pepper.

   Put turkey into covered roaster and place in unheated oven. Set temperature to 550° for 15 minutes. Lower oven temperature to 450° for 1 hour. Reduce heat to 400° for an additional hour.

   After 2 hours and 15 minutes, remove lid on roaster and baste bird with drippings. Add peeled and quartered potatoes, carrots and onions. Cook covered at 375° for about 45 minutes or until vegetables are cooked.

NORTH ITALIAN STUFFED TURKEY   ------   *Mary's Recipe*

20-pound turkey
Olive oil
2 cups California dry white wine
Salt and pepper to taste
Carrots, potatoes, celery, peeled and quartered (optional)

DRESSING:

2 cups cooked white rice, cooled
1-1/2 pounds lean ground beef
3/4 cup Romano cheese, grated
1 egg
1/4 cup olive oil
3/4 cup minced parsley
6 large garlic cloves, chopped
Salt and pepper to taste

Rinse and dry turkey. Combine ground beef, onion, rice, garlic, parsley, cheese and egg. Mix well. Stuff turkey with dressing. Rub bird with olive oil. Pour wine over turkey. Season skin of turkey with salt and pepper.

   Preheat oven to 500°. Place bird in oven for 20 minutes, tightly covering the pan. Reduce temperature to 375° and cook bird for an additional 3 to 3-1/2 hours. Carrots, potatoes, and celery pieces may be added during the last 30 minutes of cooking. More liquid, wine or water, might be needed during the cooking time.

Wine Suggestion: California Zinfandel

CRANBERRY MOLD

This colorful gelatin mold is a traditional turkey accompaniment at the Indelicato family Thanksgiving gatherings.

1 package strawberry gelatin
       (6 ounces)
1 can whole cranberry sauce
       (14 ounces)
3/4 cup chopped apples
1/2 cup chopped celery
1/3 cup chopped walnuts

Prepare gelatin as directed on package. When mixture begins to thicken, fold in cranberry sauce, apples, celery, and nuts. Refrigerate until set. Serve on lettuce leaves.

The family usually gathers at our house for Thanksgiving. We all sit around a large table that takes up almost the entire room.

   This is the same table where eleven people used to eat their daily meals: Gaspare and Caterina Indelicato, their four children and the Sam Luppino family of five who lived with them.

   Gaspare bought the big table so that everyone could be together for meals. Later, when he and Caterina built a new brick home near the winery, they left the oversized piece of furniture in the old house. Years later, Tony and I rescued the big table, refinished it, and brought it into the center of our home.

   —Mary Indelicato

Rabbit Stew

Stufato di Coniglio

Sometimes we grilled rabbit outside in the yard. Dad dug a hole and built a wood fire in it. When the wood had burned down to coals, he put a homemade grill across.

After salting and peppering the rabbit pieces, I'd put them on the grill and brush them with olive oil. Because the grill was near the garden, I grabbed a handful of mint leaves, crushed them slightly and used them as a brush. They gave a bit of mint flavor to the meat.

—Frances Indelicato Sciabica

1 rabbit (3 to 4 pounds), cut up
2 tablespoons salt
4 tablespoons olive oil
1-1/2 cups chopped onions
Salt and pepper
1 can whole tomatoes (28 ounces) with juice
4 medium potatoes, peeled and quartered
1 cup hot water
1/4 teaspoon crushed red pepper

Place rabbit pieces in a pot and cover with water. Add 2 tablespoons salt. Let stand for 2 hours, then rinse rabbit under cold tap water and dry thoroughly with paper towels.

Heat olive oil in large skillet. Sauté rabbit pieces and onion for 20 minutes. Add salt and pepper to taste and continue browning. Add tomatoes, cover and simmer 20 minutes.

Add potatoes and water. Continue simmering for about 30 minutes or until rabbit and potatoes are tender. Serves 4.

Wine Suggestion: California Sauvignon Blanc.

We ate a lot of rabbit. We had hutches behind the house with hundreds of rabbits. Sometimes I shot wild rabbits and then Mom would use those and save the tame rabbits for days when there was no other food.

She usually fried the rabbit with garlic and added potatoes. We ate so much rabbit back then that today I just don't want any.

—Tony Indelicato

Papa and Mama with their four children.

Beef and Lamb

Basic Beef Burgundy

Once a winery workhorse, this restored 1946 GMC 1.5 ton truck is now on display at our Black Stallion Estate Winery in Napa.

Upon the United States entry into World War II, civilian vehicle production was stopped and converted to military uses. One of just 36,000 produced, this 1946 flat-bed truck, from the era dubbed the "Art Deco" period, provided qualified business users with heavy-duty power and pre-war styling until full vehicle production began again in 1947.

Based upon 1941 models, the front end bears bulbous fenders, a massive 2-tier chrome grill and raised front hood resembling the sleek passenger locomotives and big factory machinery of the era.

In 1946 when gasoline was 15 cents per gallon, this truck cost about $1400 but the Indelicato Family bought it second-hand for a few hundred dollars and used it at the Manteca winery until it just stopped running. A dedicated crew of winery employees volunteered to restore this rare truck to its former glory.

3 pounds lean, stew meat, cut into 2 inch cubes
1/2 cup flour
1/2 teaspoon salt
1/8 teaspoon black pepper
2 tablespoons olive oil
6 tablespoons butter, divided
1/4 cup brandy
3 slices bacon, diced
2 cups diced onion
2 cloves garlic, minced
3/4 cup thinly sliced carrots
2 tablespoons minced parsley
1 bay leaf
1/2 teaspoon thyme
2 cups California Pinot Noir wine
12 small pearl white onions
1 teaspoon sugar
24 firm white mushroom caps
1 tablespoon butter

Dust meat cubes in flour seasoned with salt and pepper. Heat olive oil and 3 tablespoons butter in skillet and brown meat on all sides. Remove meat to casserole. Warm brandy, ignite and pour over meat.

Sauté bacon in skillet. When partially cooked, add onions, garlic and carrots and cook until limp. Add to casserole with parsley, bay leaf, thyme and wine. Cover and cook in 325° oven for 3 hours. After 2-1/2 hours of cooking, add onions which have been sautéed in butter with sugar until lightly brown.

Sauté mushrooms in butter and add during last 5 minutes of cooking. Remove casserole from oven and serve immediately.
Serves 6 to 8.

Plenty of French bread, boiled new potatoes plus a green salad with tart vinaigrette dressing complete this hearty meal. Finish with fresh fruit or a chilled lemon mousse.

Wine Suggestion: California Pinot Noir or Cabernet Sauvignon.

Beef With Mushroom Soup

3-pound piece lean, boneless beef (chuck or cross rib)
Salt and pepper to tast
½ teaspoon Italian seasoning
6 cloves garlic
1 onion, chopped
1/4 cup parsley
3 celery ribs chopped
2 carrots, halved
4 peeled white potatoes cut in half
1 tablespoon diced bacon
1 cup California Pinot Noir wine
1 can of mushroom soup (12 ounces)

Insert garlic cloves into beef roast and rub with salt and pepper. Cover the meat with the mushroom soup. Add onion, Italian seasoning, carrots, potatoes, celery and wine.

Cover with lid and cook in 350° oven for 2 hours. Cook one hour longer if you prefer your roast to be well done. Allow roast to rest 15 minutes before serving. If you prefer more gravy, add an additional cup of water to the mushroom soup.
Serves 4 to 6

Wine Suggestion: California Pinot Noir.

Nanna, holding Cheryl, 1 month old and Nonno holding 6 months old Jay with all the grandchildren in December 1960.
Middle Row: Kathy Sciabica, age 10.
Bottom Row: Joe Sciabica Jr., age 2, Frank Indelicato Jr., age 3, Robert Indelicato, age 4 and Marie Indelicato, age 5.

Francy's Beef Stew

2 pounds stew meat cut into 2-inch cubes
1/4 cup flour
2 tablespoons vegetable oil or bacon fat
1/4 cup water
1 cup California Zinfandel wine
1/4 cup flour mixed to a paste with 1/4 cup cold water
1/2 teaspoon salt
3 bay leaves
20 small whole black peppercorns
1 lemon, thinly sliced

Roll meat cubes in flour and brown in hot bacon fat or oil. Transfer to casserole. Drain fat from skillet and add water, loosening browned bits. Add wine, flour-water mixture and salt. Bring to a boil, stirring constantly until thickened. Pour liquid mixture over meat in casserole, adding bay leaves and peppercorns. Cover and cook 3 hours in 325° oven. Add lemon slices during last half hour of cooking. Serves 6.

Wine Suggestion: California Zinfandel.

Frances Indelicato Sciabica, slicing bread for another family get-together.

Dot's Beef Stew

3 pounds rump (or chuck) roast, cut into 2 inch cubes
Salt and pepper to taste
1 can tomato sauce (8 ounces)
1 can chopped mushrooms (4 ounces)
1/4 cup fresh minced parsley
6 cloves garlic, minced
1 tablespoon minced shallots (or green onions)
1/4 teaspoon each rosemary, thyme
1 onion, chopped
1 cup California Cabernet Sauvignon wine

Season meat with salt and pepper. Combine parsley, garlic, onion, shallots and herbs in a bowl. Mix well. In a 4-quart pan, brown meat, then add the bowl of chopped vegetables. Pour red wine over all.

Bring to a boil for 2 minutes, cover tightly and simmer on stove top over low heat for 2 hours or until done to your liking. Skim off fat before serving.
Serves 6 to 8.

Wine Suggestion: California Cabernet Sauvignon.

Beef With Bleu Cheese

This ground beef dish leaves behind the word "hamburger" and moves up into the steak family.

1 pound ground round beef
2 ounces ham, minced
Salt and pepper to taste
2 ounces bleu cheese
1/2 cup California dry red wine
2 tablespoons butter
Parsley for garnish

Mix ground beef with ham. Add small amount of salt and pepper. Cut cheese into 4 squares. Mold meat around cheese, forming into flattened patties. Place in shallow dish. Cover patties with wine and let stand, covered, in refrigerator about 4 hours. Place 1 tablespoon butter in pan and fry to desired doneness.

Remove patties to heated plate. Add remaining butter to wine marinade and boil on top of stove. Pour over patties. Garnish with parsley and serve. Makes 4 patties.

Wine Suggestion: California Cabernet Sauvignon.

Mary's Pot Roast

Beef roast (5 pounds)
2 tablespoons olive oil
1 onion, sliced
5 garlic cloves, sliced
1 can whole tomatoes (16 ounces)
2 cans tomato sauce (8 ounces each)
1 cup California Pinot Noir wine
2 teaspoons Italian seasoning

Brown beef on both sides in olive oil in large, flat pan. Place onions and garlic on top. Combine tomatoes, tomato sauce, wine, and Italian seasoning and pour around meat. Cover and simmer for 2 hours over low heat on stove top or bake in 325° oven. Check occasionally, adding water, if necessary.
Serves 4 to 6.

Wine Suggestion: California Pinot Noir

PINOT NOIR VALENCIA

1 part orange juice
2 parts California Pinot Noir wine
Fresh fruit
Ice cubes

Combine orange juice and wine. Stir. Add ice cubes, garnish with fruit stir and serve. For variety, add a sprig of fresh mint and a pinch of powdered sugar.
Makes a single serving.

10 SECOND SANGRIA

1 bottle 750 ml California red wine
1 bottle 750 ml Sparkling lemonade
Combine and pour over ice.
Makes 8 servings.

Young children at the 1990 Grape Stomp.

Car Show 1990 Grape Stomp.

Round Steak With Musrooms

3 pounds beef round steak
Flour with salt & pepper to taste
2 pounds fresh mushrooms, sliced
1/2 cup California dry red wine
2 cups water
2 tablespoons corn starch
2 tablespoons minced parsley
1 tablespoon minced fresh garlic or 1 tablespoon garlic powder

Pound steak with meat mallet to tenderize, cut in 2 inch squares. Dust meat with seasoned flour. Brown floured steaks on both sides. Add mushrooms, water, wine and parsley. Cook until tender.

Add 2 tablespoons of water to the corn starch and stir into a paste. Add the paste to the steak liquid to thicken gravy.
Serve hot with French bread.
Serves 4.

Wine Suggestion: California Petite Sirah

Vince Indelicato, second row, second from right, pictured with his National Guard unit at Camp Roberts near King City, California, circa 1955

"Who could have predicted that we would one day own San Bernabe Vineyards, just a few miles away." --Dorothy Indelicato

Chorizo Meatballs

Albondigas con Lukainka

Joe Larranga, retired Delicato employee, transformed the ordinary meatball into a hot number with a quarter pound of spicy sausage.

1/4 pound chorizo sausage meat, casing removed
1 pound lean ground meat
3/4 tablespoon salt
1 tablespoon minced parsley
1 can tomato sauce (8 ounces)
2 slices French bread with crust
1 egg, lightly beaten
1/4 cup flour (approximately)
4 tablespoons olive oil
1/2 cup California dry white wine
1 cup chicken stock or water

Combine the clay-red chorizo with the brown-red beef, mixing well to achieve an even color. Add salt, parsley and tomato sauce. Soak bread in small saucer of water for 2 to 3 minutes. Squeeze dry and add to meat mixture. Blend in beaten egg.

Begin forming 20 "golfball" - sized meatballs. Place flour on plate or sheet of waxed paper. Roll meatballs in flour and place in hot oil in flat skillet. When meat balls are brown on one side, carefully turn over. Shake pan to prevent meat balls from sticking.

Add wine and stock or water when meat is evenly brown. Cover and simmer for 30 minutes, shaking pan occasionally.
Serves 4

"Plenty of potatoes or rice are necessary," Joe added, "to soak up the delicious sauce."

Wine Suggestion: California Zinfandel

Each summer, Portuguese-Americans in the Manteca area observe a traditional festival that means good food, good times and most important—a chance to honor their common heritage.

The Festa (fesh-ta) commemorates the charity of Portugal's Queen Isabel, who asked the nobles of her kingdom to dedicate one day a year to the Holy Ghost. On this feast day, she proclaimed, they would give food and money to the poor.

After a parade and Catholic mass, which are part of the Festa, townspeople and Portuguese from surrounding communities enjoy a feast of traditional Portuguese foods: Sopas, sweet breads and Tremocos, (lupin beans). Joe Teicheira, one of the renowned chefs of the local festival, shares his Sopas recipe, which feeds more than 600 people (page 97).

Dorothy Cardoza Indelicato,
Little Queen of the July 1940 Festa.

Peppery Kebabs

1-1/2 pounds, boneless sirloin, cubed
3/4 cup California Zinfandel wine
2 tablespoons olive oil
1/2 teaspoon salt
1/2 large, mild yellow onion, thinly sliced
1/2 teaspoon dried thyme
2 to 3 tablespoons peppercorns

Marinate meat cubes in glass bowl with wine, oil, salt, onion and thyme for 2 to 3 hours. Crack peppercorns with flat side of knife blade and spread on flat surface. Thread steak cubes on skewers and roll lightly in pepper.

Grill over very hot charcoal, turning once, about 3 minutes on each side for medium rare. Serves 4.

Wine Suggestion: California old vine Zinfandel.

Hint: If using wooden skewers for kebabs, soak in water for one hour to prevent excessive charring.

Steak Joan

1 pound sirloin steak, about 1-inch thick
1 tablespoon peppercorns, crushed
1 tablespoon butter
1 tablespoon olive oil
2 tablespoons California dry sherry wine
2 tablespoons heavy cream
1 tablespoon Dijon mustard
Fresh parsley for garnish

Crush peppercorns and press firmly into both sides of steak. Chill for several hours.

Melt butter and oil in heavy skillet. Fry or grill steak over high heat until crisp on the outside but pink in the center. Remove to platter and keep warm while sauce is prepared.

Combine sherry, cream and mustard and add to skillet. Over low heat, stir mixture until hot. Pour over steak, garnish with parsley and serve immediately.
Makes 4 servings.

Wine Suggestion: California Zinfandel or Cabernet Sauvignon.

Portuguese Sopas

5-pound beef pot roast, cut into 3 pieces
4 cloves garlic
3 cans tomato sauce (8 ounces each)
1/2 cup onion, chopped
1/2 cup parsley, chopped
5 celery stalks, chopped
1 bottle California dry white wine (750 ml)
10 cups cold water
1 teaspoon pepper
2 tablespoons salt
1 tablespoon ground allspice
1/2 teaspoon cumin seeds
4 bay leaves
1 tablespoon red wine vinegar
1 head green cabbage, cored and quartered
1 loaf French bread, cut into 1-inch slices
25 whole fresh mint leaves with stem—essential

Combine all ingredients except mint and bread in a large pot. Cover and simmer 6 hours. During last hour, add cabbage.

At serving time, cover bottom of large, shallow serving dish with bread slices. Lay lightly bruised mint leaves on top of bread so each piece is touched by mint flavor. Ladle hot meat, cabbage and broth on top of bread and mint and eat immediately. Serves 6.

Wine suggestion: California Zinfandel

Klaire Bynum, age 5, holding a sopas spice bag. Klaire is now a Human Resources Director for Delicato Family Vineyards at our Napa office.

SOPAS FOR THE FESTA

After attending Manteca's St. Anthony's Catholic Church services, this meal is traditionally served free of charge to the community and the returning parade participants.

Pour 5 gallons cold water into a large pot. Add cheesecloth spice bag containing: 4 large handfuls bay leaves, 3 large handfuls cinnamon sticks, 2 pounds slivered bell peppers, 3 pounds pickling spice, 2-1/2 pounds Italian seasoning. Bring to a boil.

Add one whole beef (700 pounds dressed weight). Fill pot with cold water to within 12 inches of rim (about 25 gallons). Add: 6 pounds salt, 5 gallons California dry white wine, 24 pounds chopped onion, 1 pound dehydrated onion, 5 ounces vinegar, 1-1/2 pounds garlic, 1/4 pound each ground oregano, peppers, nutmeg, ground rosemary, allspice and cumin seed. 4 gallons tomato paste, 3 gallons tomato ketchup, 5 ounces Worcestershire sauce.

Cover and simmer for 15 hours. One hour before serving add 15 large heads of cabbage (halved and cored).

To serve: place slices of day old French bread and whole mint leaves in large serving pan (two hundred loaves of bread and 4000 sprigs of fresh mint are needed). Ladle hot Sopas on top.

Serves a large, hungry crowd.

Recipe courtesy of
Joe Teicheira, Manteca, California

GRAPE JELLY

10 cups grape juice*
2 packages pectin (1.75 ounces each)
    (Sure Jell works well)
1 tablespoon butter
½ cup lemon juice
12 cups sugar

Set out the utensils that you will need for the recipe: Large 8 quart pan, small pan, jars, rings, lids, jelly funnel, measuring cups, sugar, juice, pectin.

Prepare and measure juice needed. Add ¼ cup lemon juice per recipe. Add 1 tablespoon of butter to minimize foaming.

In a small pot bring water to just below boiling point. Place the amount of lids needed in the water and keep the water temperature just below boiling.

Place pectin (Sure Jell) in the juice and stir. Bring juice to a boil. Place the measured sugar (12 cups) into the boiling juice. Wait for juice to boil once more after sugar has been added. Be sure it is a rolling boil. Boil for one minute. Turn off heat source. Remove foam.

Use a ladle and funnel to pour jelly into jars. Fill to about 1/4 inch from top of jar. Wipe the rim of the jar before sealing. The lids will make a popping sound as the jelly jars cool and seal.

Label jar with variety of jelly and date. Store jelly jars at room temperature away from a heat source. After jar has been opened. Store unused jelly in refrigerator. Makes: 16 (8 ounces) jars.

Wine can be substituted to make wine jelly

Lamb Chops

4 lamb chops (about 5 ounces each)
½ cup grape jelly (see sidebar recipe)
6 tablespoons California medium-dry sherry wine
4 orange strips*
Orange wedges for garnish

Broil chops, turning once, until crisp on outside, but still pink in center. Combine jelly, sherry and orange strips. Cook until hot and jelly dissolves. Place chops on heated serving platter and spoon sauce over chops. Garnish with orange wedges. Serves 4.

Wine Suggestion: California Pinot Grigio.

Using knife or peeler, cut a ½-inch strip of orange peel from top to bottom of orange. Avoid cutting into white membrane, which is bitter.

Generation four, Danton Indelicato, learning to make grape jelly.

Shish Kebabs

The red wine marinade makes a difference. Use it for other lamb dishes as well.

2 pounds lamb cut into 1-inch cubes
16 medium whole mushrooms
1 large green pepper, cut into 1-inch chunks
2 medium onions, peeled and quartered
2 medium tomatoes, quartered

MARINADE:

1/4 cup olive oil
3/4 cup California dry red wine
1 onion, chopped
1 clove garlic, chopped
1/4 teaspoon basil
1/4 teaspoon marjoram
1/4 teaspoon rosemary
1 teaspoon salt
1/8 teaspoon pepper

Combine all marinade ingredients in a glass bowl. Add lamb cubes and refrigerate, covered, for 8 hours, preferably overnight.

To cook, place lamb on skewers and grill 15 to 20 minutes, turning occasionally and basting twice with marinade. Wipe mushrooms with damp cloth and parboil green pepper pieces for added tenderness, if desired. Arrange vegetables on 4 separate skewers and grill for the last 10 minutes, turning often and basting frequently with marinade.
Serves 4.

Hint: If using wood skewers, soak in water for one hour to prevent charring.

Wine Suggestion: California Zinfandel.

CORN BAKED IN FOIL
Corn is ready when it turns a vivid yellow. Serve with Shish Kebabs.

1 cob of corn, husked
1/2 teaspoon butter
1/2 teaspoon horseradish
1/2 teaspoon Dijon mustard
Dash of salt
Dash of white pepper

Mix all ingredients and smear on corn. Wrap loosely in foil. Bake for 30 minutes in 450° oven or on grill. If grilling, check occasionally to avoid scorching and add dash of water if completely dry.

Black Stallion Estate Winery in the Oak Knoll district of Napa Valley was purchased by the Indelicato family in 2010.

Lamb With Orange

1-1/2 pounds boneless lamb cut into 2 inch cubes
Salt and pepper to taste
2 teaspoons powdered thyme
4 tablespoons olive oil, divided
1-1/2 cups California dry white wine
2-1/2 cups thinly sliced white onions
2 cups peeled potatoes, cut into 1/2-inch slices
1 tablespoon slivered garlic, lightly bruised
4 1-inch wide strips of fresh orange rind
2 bay leaves
1/2 cup small black olives (Greek Calamata are best)
4 tablespoons finely minced fresh parsley for garnish

Sprinkle lamb cubes with salt, pepper and thyme. Heat 2 tablespoons olive oil in heavy pan. Add lamb and sauté until browned. Remove meat to bowl.

Add wine to pan, scraping up browned bits on bottom of pan, and pour into bowl with lamb.

Heat 2 more tablespoons olive oil in same pan. Add onions, potatoes, garlic and orange rind. Cook for 5 minutes then add bay leaves, lamb and wine. Simmer over very low heat for 1 hour or until potatoes are done.

Check seasonings. Remove bay leaves and orange rind. Add olives during last 5 minutes of cooking. Garnish with parsley. Serves 6.

Wine Suggestion: California Pinot Noir.

Leg Of Lamb

1 leg of lamb (about 4 to 5 pounds)
2 cups California dry white wine
1 onion, sliced
2 garlic cloves, halved
2 bay leaves
Salt
Freshly ground black pepper
4 bacon strips

For a marinade, combine wine, onion, garlic and bay leaves. Marinate lamb for several hours. Place lamb in a roaster, reserving marinade.

Sprinkle salt and black pepper on lamb and rub into meat. Place bacon strips over lamb and roast uncovered in 325° oven 30 to 35 minutes per pound, basting with reserved marinade.
Serves 8

Wine Suggestion: California Cabernet Sauvignon.

Ox Tail Stew

5 pounds beef ox tail
2 tablespoons olive oil
1 can diced tomatoes (14 ounces)
1 cup California dry red wine
1 medium yellow onion, quartered
1 tablespoon granulated garlic
8 ounces fresh mushrooms, sliced
4 medium red potatoes, in halves
10 sweet green peppers, quartered, stems and seeds removed
Salt and pepper to taste

In a large skillet, heat olive oil and brown meat on all sides, about 20 minutes. Set aside meat, remove fat and grease, then return meat to skillet.

Increase heat to highest setting and add tomatoes, including liquid, onions, garlic and wine. Season with salt and pepper to taste and bring to a boil.

Cover and reduce heat to lowest setting. Cook for 5 hours or until meat falls off the bones.

Add potatoes, peppers and mushrooms. Stir, cover and cook approximately one more hour or until vegetables are done.
Serves 4

Son-in-law, Kim Mathews, contributed this recipe and recommends serving over creamy polenta. (see page 104)

Wine Suggestion: California Cabernet Sauvignon.

Third generation management: Chris Indelicato (CEO) left and Jay Indelicato (COO).

Veal With Brandy Cream

4 slices veal (about 6 ounces each)
Flour for dusting
2 tablespoons unsalted butter
4 tablespoons olive oil
2 tablespoons chopped shallots
1-1/4 cups beef broth
1/4 cup brandy
3/4 cup fresh mushrooms, thinly sliced
1/2 cup heavy cream
1 teaspoon cornstarch
2 tablespoons water

To tenderize, place veal between two sheets of waxed paper and pound with a meat mallet.

Lightly dust in flour. Over medium heat, sauté veal in olive oil for 3 minutes one side and 2 minutes on the other. Place veal on warm platter.

In same oil add 2 tablespoons of butter and sauté shallots for approximately one minute. Add beef broth and boil for 4 minutes. Add brandy and mushrooms and boil an additional minute.

Dissolve cornstarch in water. Add mixture with cream to pan. Stir continuously until sauce thickens. Place veal slices in sauce and heat to serve. Makes 4 portions.

Wine Suggestion: California Moscato or Pinot Grigio

The barrel room of Delicato's Monterey County winery.

Veal In Champagne

4 thin, boneless veal slices (about 6 ounces each)
Flour for dusting
4 tablespoons olive oil
2 tablespoons unsalted butter
4 thin, unpeeled lemon slices (rounds)
1 avocado, peeled, sliced thinly lengthwise
2 tablespoons chopped shallots
1/4 cup lemon juice
3/4 cup extra-dry sparkling wine

To tenderize, place veal between two sheets of wax paper and pound with a meat mallet. Lightly dust with flour. Sauté veal in olive oil over medium heat for 3 minutes on one side and 2 minutes of the other. Place on warm platter. Place lemon rounds on veal. Lay 4 to 5 avocado slices in fan design over each lemon round.

Wipe pan with paper towels then melt 2 tablespoons butter over medium heat. Quickly sauté shallots. Add lemon juice and champagne and boil for 1 minute, stirring continually.
Pour sauce over veal and serve immediately.

Surround this entreé with new potatoes, buttered asparagus, and salad greens.

Wine Suggestion: California Chardonnay.

Osso Buco

Ask your butcher for veal shanks if you don't see them in the case. An interesting variation in meal planning.

4 veal shin bones, 1-1/2 inch thick, 7 to 10 ounces each
1/4 cup flour
Salt and pepper to taste
2 tablespoons olive oil
2 tablespoons butter
1/2 cup minced carrot
1/2 cup minced onion
1/2 cup minced celery
1 bay leaf
1/2 teaspoon thyme
1 piece lemon peel (1/2 x 3 inches)
1 tomato, skinned, diced and seeded, about 1/2 cup
   (1 tablespoon tomato paste may be substituted)
1/2 cup beef broth
1 cup California dry white wine
Gremolata

Dredge bones in flour seasoned with salt and pepper. Melt oil and butter and brown meat evenly. Remove to platter.

In same pan, sauté carrot, onion and celery until soft. Add bay leaf, thyme, lemon peel and tomato. Return meat to pan.

Add broth and wine to meat. Bring to a boil. Reduce heat and simmer covered for 1-1/2 hours or until meat loosens and almost falls from bones. Remove bay leaf and lemon peel. Before serving, sprinkle with gremolata and simmer 5 minutes to meld flavors. Serves 4.

GREMOLATA:

1/3 cup minced parsley
2 cloves garlic, finely minced
2 teaspoons lemon rind

Combine freshly prepared ingredients and stir into hot veal dish.

Traditionally Osso Buco is served with a risotto. Steamed rice is quicker and compliments the meal just as well.

Wine Suggestion: California Sauvignon Blanc.

As we married and had families, we all worked around the winery, especially during the busy crush time.

The children helped, too. Robert remembers standing on a box when he was only six years old to check empty bottles on the bottling line. A year later he drove a forklift, even though he could barely reach the clutch. Joe Sciabica, Jr. recalls driving a tractor to dump stems and pumice in the fields when he was only seven. His sister Kathy helped in the bottling room, putting on seals.

By 1975, all of Gaspare's grandchildren had jobs at the winery. Michael helped in the tasting room, Frank, Jay, Robert and Chris were in maintenance, and Cheryl and Marie worked in the office.

Today the children are part of the management team after graduating with college degrees.

—Dorothy Indelicato

I remember my first job at the winery at about age five: putting a month's worth of paid invoices in alphabetical order for my mom to file. At first it seemed pretty fun but it didn't take long for me to whine: "I'm bored."

—Marie Indelicato Mathews

Note:
When my children became bored they were required to do calisthenics until they were no longer "bored".

—Dorothy Indelicato

Braised Beef Short Ribs

6 pounds beef short ribs, cut into equal portions
1/4 cup olive oil
2 cups yellow onions, diced
2 cups celery, diced
2 cups carrots peeled, diced
2 tablespoons parsley, finely chopped
2 tablespoons basil, finely chopped
1 tablespoon rosemary leaves, finely chopped
2 tablespoons thyme leaves, finely chopped
2 tablespoons sage leaves, finely chopped
2 tablespoons oregano leaves, finely chopped
4 garlic cloves, finely chopped
3 cans chopped tomatoes (8 ounces each)
1 can tomato paste (6 ounces)
1 cup California dry red wine
1 cup California dry white wine
2 quarts beef stock
1/4 cup balsamic vinegar
Kosher salt and ground pepper to taste
All-purpose flour to dredge the meat

Fourth Generation Stephen Mathews eating grapes instead of stomping them.

Preheat oven to 350°. Season flour with salt and pepper and lightly dredge meat. Heat olive oil in a braising pan. Place short ribs into the pan and sear evenly. Remove from pan and reserve.

Add the vegetables to the pan and sauté until lightly caramelized. Add the tomato paste and incorporate, being careful not to burn. Deglaze pan with red and white wines. Add all herbs, diced tomatoes, balsamic vinegar, and beef stock. Bring to a boil.

Return the short ribs to the pan, cover and place in the heated oven for 90 minutes. Turn the short ribs and return to the oven for another 90 minutes. Serves 6

Serve over creamy polenta

Creamy Polenta

4 cups warm water
1 cup yellow corn meal
1 teaspoon salt
3 tablespoon butter

Bring water to a boil, add salt. Slowly whisk corn meal into the boiling water. Continue whisking until the polenta thickens. Reduce heat to low and cook until tender, about 15 minutes. Turn off heat, add butter and stir until melted.

Cook the polenta for 30-40 minutes.

Left over polenta can be made creamy again by stirring in a little warm broth, milk, or water on lowest heat setting.

Pork

Family Sausages

Every winter we made sausage. We children cried during the slaughtering because we had raised the pig and became fond of the animal. But it was a busy day and soon we'd be in the middle of the sausage-making excitement and forget our sadness.

Mom knew a lot about pigs from growing up in Italy. Her blood sausage made with pine nuts, Cream of Wheat and orange peel was a favorite. It tasted a little like mincemeat.

She also rolled up hot chili pepper and fennel in strips of pig skin, tied them with string, and air-cured them. Later, she would boil and slice the "hot pork" for snacks or lunch.

Today we still make the sausage from the same recipe, only now we get the ground pork from a butcher. When we were children, the sausages were cured and then packed in pork lard in gallon olive oil cans to preserve them. We didn't have a refrigerator or even an ice box. Today, we cure the sausages for a few days and then freeze them.

When the folks were first married, Dad heard that beef could be added to the traditional all-pork sausage. Even though Mom protested, he tried the combination. Mom said they buried a lot of sausage that year and loved to tell the story. After that, we stuck to the original recipe.

When we were growing up, these sausages were a mainstay of our diet. We'd come home hungry from school and barbecue a few on the ashes in the pot-bellied wood stove. Sometimes we'd throw whole garlic heads onto the coals and let them cook until they softened. Then we'd squirt them hot onto bread slices to eat with the sizzling sausage.

Now, once a year, usually the second Saturday of January, the family gathers in the basement of the old homestead to make sausage. The ground pork, about 300 pounds, is heaped onto an oil cloth covered table. The men measure out the chili peppers, salt and anise seeds and take turns blending the ingredients with their hands.

— Tony Indelicato

Fourth generations making sausage. 2014.

We start washing the natural casings with water and lemons early in the afternoon. About six o'clock, the family starts to arrive, carrying food for a potluck supper. Wine is set out and a sample of the sausage meat is sautéed.

Tasting the spicy sausage meat is the high point of the evening. There are always exaggerated gestures of pain and good-natured arguments about whether it is hot enough.

Dad used to say he had to make the sausage spicy or we kids would eat up a year's supply in a week. After we've filled up on the spiced meat, beans, salads, casseroles, bread and wine, we get to work.

The men handle the sausage stuffer. As sausages come off the machine, one of the family members ties the links and tosses them to the group waiting at the tables, where each link is pierced thoroughly with a fork. The children especially like this task.

Frank supervises the hanging of the sausages. At one end of the basement, he carefully covers boards with white paper, then hangs the completed sausages up to cure.

There's plenty of time to talk as we are together for five to six hours. The little ones get tired and sometimes curl up to sleep. The older children often bring their dates. (Maybe it's a good way to see if they'll fit into the family.)

After the sausages are made, the desserts are uncovered and served with coffee. It's nearly midnight when the last person leaves and the light is turned off. Two days later everyone will return to the house and claim a share of the sausage.

— Vince Indelicato

Sausage Party, 2014.

Family Sausages - Clan Size

For the fainthearted, use half as much chili pepper.

1 package (hank) casings
3 oranges or lemons, sliced
100 pounds coarsely ground pork butt (35 percent fat)
3 ounces crushed chili pepper
2 pounds salt
3 pounds mild California chili pods (ancho or cubanelle peppers),
  stems removed, coarsely gound
3 cups anise seeds
Kitchen string
Plus at least 2 dozen helping hands!

Freshen casings by soaking in cold water with orange or lemon slices. Wash off salt and cut into 36" pieces.

   Mix meat with crushed chili peppers, salt, ground chili pods and anise seed. Test sausage for the proper amount of seasonings by frying some in a skillet. At this point, you may shape some sausage into individual breakfast patties separated with paper and freeze.

   Fill casings with meat and tie off each end with kitchen string. Pierce sausages all over with fork tines and hang in a cool place for 24 hours.

   This is fresh sausage, made with uncooked meat and not smoked or cured after filling. It must be frozen immediately after the hanging time or refrigerated and eaten within 3 days. Makes approximately 65, 36-inch links.

Sausage Party, 1985.

Family Sausages - Family Size

Just enough for the family.

5 casings
1 lemon, sliced
8 pounds coarsely ground pork butt (35% fat)
1 tablespoon crushed chili pepper
5 teaspoons salt
3 ounces mild California chili pods (stems removed, coarsely ground*)
4 tablespoons anise seed
Kitchen string

Follow directions for the larger recipe. Makes about 5, 36-inch links.

*The drier the peppers are, the easier they are to grind.

COOKING THE SAUSAGE

Each family member takes home a share of the sausage and cooks it differently. All agree, however, that the sausage tastes best grilled over charcoal or oven broiled.

Alice Indelicato and Frances Indelicato Sciabica usually broil frozen sausages right from the freezer.

Mary Indelicato likes to defrost the sausages in the microwave oven then broil them.

I defrost the sausages quickly in the microwave oven or slowly in the refrigerator. If I broil them frozen, halfway through cooking, I will split the sausages lengthwise and lay them skin side down, so the inside gets thoroughly cooked.

— Dorothy Indelicato

RED WINE MUSTARD

Rosy in color, this condiment is a pleasant surprise on ham, sausage or liverwurst.

1/4 cup mustard seeds
1/4 cup California dry red wine
1/3 cup red wine vinegar
1/4 cup water
1/2 teaspoon honey
1/4 teaspoon ground allspice
1/4 teaspoon black pepper
1 teaspoon finely minced garlic
1-1/2 teaspoons coarse kosher salt
1 bay leaf, finely crumbled

Combine the mustard seeds, wine and wine vinegar in a dish, and let stand for 3 hours. Do not extend time or seeds will absorb too much liquid.

Place water, honey, allspice, pepper, garlic, salt and bay leaf in blender and whirl to a coarse texture. Put mixture in top of double boiler. Stir over simmering water for 5 to 10 minutes or until the mustard has thickened somewhat, but is not as thick as prepared mustard. Scrape mixture into a jar, let cool and refrigerate.
Makes 3/4 to 1 cup.

Great-Grandmas, Amelia Pauletto and Mary Cardoza, advising the sausage makers.

Ham Baked In Wine

ONIONS IN WINE

A cool, refreshing relish to serve with ham.

4 cups Vidalia onions, thinly sliced
1 teaspoon salt
1/8 teaspoon white pepper
2 cups California dry white wine
Parsley sprigs for garnish

Place onions, salt and pepper in wine and chill for several hours or overnight. Garnish with parsley sprigs. Makes 4 cups.

Variation: For a brighter, rosier look, substitute red onions and Cabernet Sauvignon; use plenty of freshly grated black pepper.

1 ham (8-pound canned or precooked)
½ bottle cream sherry wine

Preheat oven to 350°. Place ham in baking pan and pour wine over it. Roast according to directions, basting frequently. Let rest for at least 15 minutes before slicing. Delicious hot or cold. Garnish with spiced apples or Cranberry Apples.

Wine Suggestion: California Pinot Noir

Cranberry Apples

Dress up your presentation with this tasty fruit garnish.

1 large baking apple per person
   (Rome beauty, Golden Delicious, Jonathan, McIntosh)
1 can whole cranberry sauce (12 ounces)
1/3 cup California Moscato wine per apple
1 orange, sliced
Cinnamon

Core apples to within 1/2 inch from bottom. Carefully slice off bottom, allowing apples to stand upright in baking dish. Fill apple centers with cranberry sauce.

Place apples next to one another in dish so apples remain upright. Pour Moscato over apples and sprinkle liberally with cinnamon. Bake in 350° oven for about 30 minutes, basting with wine several times. Near end of baking time, test apples for doneness. Apples should be soft, but not mushy.

Let apples cool a few minutes, then slice in half through cranberry center. Place apple halves on serving platter, skin side down. Spoon baking liquid over apples and garnish platter with orange slices.

Serve hot or cold.

Pork Chops With Fennel

An easy sauce makes itself while these chops simmer. The fennel seeds add a pleasant, new taste.

4 pork chops (1/2-inch thick)
2 tablespoons olive oil
3 to 4 cloves garlic
Salt and pepper to taste
1/4 teaspoon fennel seeds
3/4 cup California dry red wine

Heat oil in skillet. Brown garlic and remove from heat. Rub chops with salt, pepper and fennel seeds. Fry chops on both sides until brown. Add red wine and cook uncovered until chops are tender. Spoon sauce over chops. Serves 4.

Accent the fennel flavor with a fresh finocchio and red radish salad. Creamed potatoes or baked potatoes are good wintertime additions. In summer, corn on the cob is colorful and easy.

Wine Suggestion: California Zinfandel or Chardonnay.

Sausage Party, 1990. Piercing the sausage with forks are Marie Indelicato Mathews, Mary Indelicato and Leslie Bloudoff.

Pork And Sage Supper

Sage is the dominant flavor. Small portions served with ample helpings of wild rice are satisfying.

3 pounds pork loin or shoulder
Freshly ground pepper to taste
4 tablespoons olive oil
2 medium onions, chopped
4 teaspoons sage
2 bay leaves
1/3 cup finely chopped parsley
1 teaspoon thyme
3/4 cup California dry white wine
1/2 cup hot water
1/2 cup dry white vermouth wine
1/3 cup capers

Trim fat and bones from meat and cut into 1-inch cubes. Sprinkle with pepper. Heat oil in large skillet and brown pork cubes on all sides.

Lower heat. Add onions, sage, bay leaves, parsley and thyme. Stir well. Add wine and hot water. Cover and simmer for 1 hour stirring occasionally and adding more white wine to maintain liquid level.

Remove meat to heated platter. Add vermouth to skillet and boil a few minutes, scraping up browned parts. Return meat to pan and add capers. Simmer to reheat. Serves 6.

Serve with wild rice, salad greens mixed with walnuts and orange slices. Corn bread with lemon butter adds a nice finish to the meal.

Wine Suggestion: California Pinot Noir

2015 Sausage Party.

Sweet And Sour Pork

2 pounds pork spare ribs, flanken cut (cut between bones)
Salt and pepper to taste
2 cloves garlic, slivered
2 tablespoons oil
1 cup water
½ cup California dry white wine
1 can pineapple chunks (13-1/2 ounces)
1 cup pineapple juice reserved from can
2 tablespoons soy sauce
3 tablespoons wine vinegar
2 tablespoons cornstarch
3/4 cup coarsely chopped green pepper (1/2 x 1-inch pieces)

Season pork with salt and pepper. Heat oil in skillet over medium heat. Brown pork with garlic. Reduce heat, add water and wine. Cover and simmer 30 minutes. Mix pineapple juice, soy sauce, vinegar and cornstarch until smooth. Add mixture to meat. Cook until sauce is clear and thickened.

Stir in pineapple chunks and green pepper pieces. Cook uncovered for 5 minutes, stirring occasionally. Serve over steamed white rice.
Serves 4.

Wine Suggestion: California Cabernet Sauvignon or Chardonnay

Chardonnay Mint Juleps

1 bundle of fresh mint
1 cup sugar
1 bottle ginger beer (12 oz.)
1 bottle California Chardonnay (750 ml)

Make a simple syrup with sugar and water in a pot and heat on high. Stir occasionally and when water begins to boil, turn off the heat and stir sugar until completely dissolved.

Prepare the mint while waiting for the water to boil . Separate the lower leaves from the stem to stir into the simple syrup. Keep the top sprigs to garnish the drink later. Stir prepped mint leaves into the simple syrup and place in the refrigerator for two to three hourss.

Strain the syrup to remove the mint leaves. Pour one ounce of mint simple syrup and 5 ounces of Chardonnay over ice into a tall glass. Add a generous splash of ginger beer on top and garnish with a fresh mint sprig.

Note: The Chardonnay Mint Juleps are served to our Club Members at Black Stallion Estate Winery while they watch the Kentucky Derby on TV Projection screens.

Left to Right: Tony Indelicato, Mike Lavieri, Ed Cardoza,Vince and Dorothy Indelicato — Filling the casings at the sausage party, 1985.

113

Chops With Wild Rice

Parsley plus the earthy flavors of pine nuts and
wild rice make this naturally good.

2 slices bacon
4 pork chops
2 cups cooked wild rice
3 tablespoons finely minced green onions
4 tablespoons pine nuts (may substitute pecans but not walnuts)
2 tablespoons minced parsley
1/2 cup California dry white wine
2 tablespoons orange zest
1 teaspoon chervil or French parsley

Cook wild rice until moist per package directions.

Fry bacon slices, reserving 2 tablespoons grease. Crumble bacon into small pieces
and set aside. Fry pork chops in bacon drippings until crisp on both sides. Place in
single layer in oven proof casserole dish.

Combine hot rice with bacon pieces, onions, pine nuts, parsley, wine, orange zest
and chervil. Mix well and spread over pork chops. Cover and bake 1 hour at 325°.
Check occasionally, adding more wine if necessary. Serves 4.

Wine Suggestions: California Pinot Grigio.

In 1992, third generation Chris Indelicato is
teaching fourth generation Stephen Mathews
how to pierce the sausage which helps the
curing process.

Frank Indelicato hanging sausages to cure in January, 1985.

Vegetables

Brocolli In White Wine

Go ahead and increase the garlic, if you like. The sauce is good on other vegetables, including boiled potatoes.

1 large head of broccoli
1/2 cup California dry white wine
3 tablespoons olive oil
2 garlic cloves, slivered
2 tablespoons lemon juice
2 tablespoons minced parsley

Wash broccoli, removing leaves, trimming flowerettes, and cutting stems into 1/2-inch pieces. Steam stem pieces until almost tender (about 15 minutes). Add flowerettes to stems and steam until both are tender but not mushy (about 5 minutes).

In separate small saucepan, simmer wine, olive oil, garlic, lemon juice and parsley for 10 minutes. Place broccoli in heated serving bowl. Pour hot sauce over vegetable and toss lightly. Serve immediately. Makes 4 to 6 portions.

Wine Suggestion: California Chardonnay

In the seventies we brothers formed a corporation and renamed the winery Delicato Vineyards. How we wish Dad and Mom could have been at the dedications of the new buildings in 1975 and 1983. They could have never imagined these buildings, especially the tower, would spring up where Dad once tended to his large garden.

— Vince Indelicato

Original architectural rendering, 1975.

The Indelicato brothers: Frank, Vincent and Anthony.

Ana's Portuguese Fava Beans

1 pound fresh fava beans, shelled
3 teaspoons salt
¾ cup olive oil
¼ cup wine vinegar
1 red onion, finely chopped
1 cup minced parsley, fresh preferred
½ teaspoon pepper (black or chili)
½ teaspoon red pepper
½ teaspoon garlic powder

Boil beans until soft, approximately 45 minutes Add salt 10 minutes before beans
have finished cooking. Drain water. Add olive oil and mix thoroughly. Add the rest
of the ingredients and mix well. Ana's Portuguese family serves these beans either
cold or at room temperature.
Serves 6.

Sweet And Sour Onions

1 tablespoon olive oil
1 tablespoon butter
2 pounds peeled red onions, cut into 1/4-inch slices
2 whole cloves
3/4 cup California dry white wine
4 tablespoons red wine vinegar
2 teaspoons sugar
Salt to taste

Heat oil and butter in heavy skillet (not aluminum). Sauté onions and cloves until
onions begin to brown and turn soft. Combine 1/2 cup wine, 2 tablespoons vinegar,
2 teaspoons sugar and add to onions.

Reduce heat, cover and simmer for 20 minutes, stirring often. Add remaining
1/4 cup wine if needed. Transfer onions to heated serving platter. Add remaining
2 tablespoons vinegar to pan, boil a minute, and pour over onions. Serve at room
temperature. This dish can be prepared the day before serving.
Serves 6.

Portuguese Beans

Portuguese beans are traditionally served at the January Sausage Party. This recipe needs to be doubled in order to feed our entire group of workers.

Jay Indelicato and Ed Cardoza, Jr.
Sausage Party, 2013.

1 pound pinto beans
5 cups water
2 tablespoons minced dried parsley
1 teaspoon chili pepper
1 tablespoon minced dried onion
½ teaspoon cumin
1 can tomato sauce (8 ounces)
1 large onion, finely chopped
1 green bell pepper, chopped
6 slices bacon
½ pound of ground beef, optional (sausage or linguica may also be used)
1 tablespoon salt

Wash beans and remove any foreign matter. Soak overnight or for at least eight hours in enough cold water to cover beans plus one inch. Drain water and rinse beans again.*

Put beans in a crock pot with water. Add parsley, pepper, onion, cumin, and tomato sauce and stir. Cook on low for about four hours until beans are soft, but not mushy.

Chop bacon into ¼ inch widths and fry until crisp. Add bacon to beans, reserving the fat. Fry the finely cut onion and bell pepper until onion is transparent. Add the onion and bell pepper and all of the bacon fat to the beans. Add salt. Stir.

If the beans do not have enough liquid add water; if the beans have too much liquid, add corn starch for a gravy-like consistency.

If meat is used, fry the meat until almost fully cooked then add to the beans. Simmer at least 30 more minutes.
Serves 8.

Serve with French bread, garlic bread, and Italian sausage.

*Quick Soak: Wash beans and remove foreign matter. To one pound of pinto beans (about 2 cups) add 8 cups of cold water. Bring water to a boil; boil for 2 minutes. Remove from heat, cover and let stand for one hour. Drain water and rinse beans again.

Sherried Asparagus

For a light wintertime supper, cut asparagus into chunks and ladle with sauce over split baked potatoes.

4 tablespoons butter, divided
1/2 cup fresh mushrooms, thickly sliced
2 tablespoons flour
1 cup half-and-half cream
Salt to taste
1/4 teaspoon dry mustard
3 tablespoons California dry sherry wine
1 pound asparagus spears, cooked al dente
1/2 cup slivered almonds, toasted
1/3 cup grated Parmesan cheese

Over low heat, sauté mushrooms briefly in butter. Remove and add additional 2 tablespoons butter to same skillet. Gently stir in flour, making a roux. Cook at least 3 minutes, then slowly whisk in cream. Add salt, mustard and sherry. Cook until thickened.

Place asparagus in a shallow baking dish. Top with almonds and mushrooms. Pour sauce over all and sprinkle cheese on last. Place under broiler until cheese is melted and bubbly. Serves 4.

Accompany with crisp cole slaw and ham slices.

Wine Suggestion: California Pinot Noir.

Patience Makes a Good Roux ...

A perfect sauce takes time at the start. You can assure a good roux by gently and continually stirring equal amounts of butter and flour over low heat for at least 3 minutes. Low heat prevents the flour from burning. Constant stirring distributes the heat, allowing the starch granules to swell evenly so they can absorb the liquid that you will add in the next step.

Herbed Cabbage

Spoon this creamy vegetable into a big baked potato for a light, meatless supper.

6 cups shredded cabbage, loosely packed
2 tablespoons butter
1/2 teaspoon salt
1/4 teaspoon white pepper
1 tablespoon pesto (see page 61)
1/2 cup California dry white wine

Melt butter in large skillet or wok. Add cabbage and toss until limp. Add salt, pepper, pesto and wine. Cover and simmer until tender, about 15 minutes. Just before serving, turn heat high for a few minutes to evaporate moisture. Serve hot. Serves 4 to 6.

Wine Suggestion: California Chardonnay

Red Pepper Gratin

Dad was a farmer. He didn't set out to be a winemaker. He borrowed money to buy 68 acres in 1924 so he could grow food for his family and earn his living farming. It was rolling land, mostly dairy fields. Bit by bit he leveled it and began to plant. His gardens were near the house. One of the gardens was exactly where our conference room is now. Sometimes on warm, sunny days when we sit inside and talk facts and figures, we all miss that earlier simplicity.

Dad's vegetable garden was the envy of everyone around here. He planted grapes, walnuts, almonds, figs, onions, garlic, cranberry beans, green beans, lettuce, carrots, peaches, apricots—even artichokes.

And lots of chicory, which he loved and grew till the day he died. He also planted prickly pears to remind him of Sicily. People who knew about the pears would sometimes stop and ask Dad if they could have a few.

The Manteca area was like a Little Sicily for Dad. The warm weather, the sandy loam soil and the crops were like the Old Country. "You can leave Manteca and go to Sicily and hardly know you've left California," he said.

— Tony Indelicato

.5 tablespoons olive oil, divided
6 large ripe tomatoes, cut into 1/4-inch rounds
3 red bell peppers, chopped into 1/2-inch pieces
1 cup fresh parsley, chopped
2/3 cup fresh basil chopped
Freshly ground pepper
1/2 cup California dry white wine
2 tablespoons capers, drained
1/2 cup unseasoned bread crumbs

Heat oven to 400°. Grease a glass casserole dish with 1 tablespoon oil. Cover the bottom with 6 or 8 tomato rounds. Sprinkle with one third of chopped bell peppers. Combine parsley, basil and pepper. Add a layer of herb mixture on top of peppers.

Repeat 2 additional layers, ending with herbs. Pour wine over mixture. Combine capers with bread crumbs and spread on top. Drizzle olive oil over all. Bake uncovered for 20 minutes or until top is lightly brown. Delicious hot or chilled for several hours—even good cold the next day. Serves 4 to 6.

Wine Suggestion: California Zinfandel.

Children of founders, 1937.
From left to right: Sam Luppino, Virginia Luppino, Vince Indelicato, Tony Indelicato (driver), Frank Indelicato, Antonio Luppino. (Frances Indelicato not included in picture.)

Sherried Sweet Potatoes

Lightly sweet potatoes accented with orange zest.

6 medium sweet potatoes (about 3 pounds)
3 tablespoons butter
2 tablespoons grated orange rind
3/4 cup California medium-dry sherry wine
Butter to grease casserole
Cinnamon and nutmeg to taste

Cook potatoes until done but not mushy. Peel and slice into a bowl. Mash with mixer or food processor, adding butter and orange rind. Add sherry and stir well. Sprinkle with cinnamon and nutmeg. Bake covered at 350° for 30 minutes or until heated through. Serves 4 to 6.

Squash Cups

1/2 small acorn squash per serving
1 tablespoon brown sugar per serving
1 tablespoon curried walnut pieces per serving
1 tablespoon California cream sherry wine per serving
Butter

Cut acorn squash in half, removing seeds and shreds. Salt lightly and bake cut side down on cookie sheet in 350° oven until done but not mushy. Turn halves cut side up in casserole dish. Sprinkle each with sugar, walnuts and sherry. Dot with butter and bake 10 additional minutes.

Variation: For a one-dish meal, sauté ground beef with a touch of onion. Mix curried nuts, salt and pepper and fill center of squash. Bake until hot.

CURRIED WALNUTS:

Place broken walnut pieces on cookie sheet. Sprinkle lightly with olive oil, salt and curry powder. Bake in 150-200° oven until crunchy and slightly brown. Cool before adding to squash recipe.

Wine Suggestion: California Zinfandel.

Every summer, Vince, Mom, Dad and I would take our children plus their five cousins to Pacific Grove to spend a week with my grandfather. This wonderful, patient man was in his eighties by then but he still had the energy to teach them how to fish from the rocks with bamboo poles. The kids caught eels, crabs, snails, and small perch from the ocean -- just across the street from my grandfather's two story house. It was often the only vacation we took each year and all of us have fond memories of those special summers we spent together.
— Dorothy Indelicato

Road Trip! Indelicato cousins pose.
Front: Chris, Mike, Cheryl
Middle: Robert, Marie, Dorothy
Back: Joe and Mary Cardoza, Jay and Frank, Jr.

Vegetable Kebabs

Grill alongside meat and poultry.

Assorted fresh vegetables: onions, green and red peppers, mushrooms,
  zucchini, eggplant, summer squash, etc.
1/2 cup olive oil
1/3 cup tarragon vinegar
1 tablespoon finely minced parsley
Salt and pepper to taste

Chop vegetables into 1-inch squares or rounds and thread on bamboo or metal skewers. Place in shallow dish.

Mix olive oil, vinegar, parsley and salt and pepper. Pour over kebabs and let marinate for at least 2 hours, turning kebabs once.

Grill in oven or over charcoal fire, brushing kebabs with marinade and turning often. Cook until tender. Remaining marinade may be heated with a dab of butter and used as a sauce to pour over cooked vegetables.

Hint: If using wood skewers, soak in water for one hour to prevent charring.

Red Cabbage

Simmered slowly in wine, this year-round vegetable accompanies
chicken and meat in a tasty way.

1 medium head red cabbage
4 slices bacon, chopped
2 medium tart apples, thinly sliced
1/4 teaspoon caraway seeds (optional)
1/4 cup cider vinegar
1/3 cup brown sugar (or 2 tablespoons honey)
Dash salt
1 cup California Zinfandel wine

Remove tough outer leaves and hard core from cabbage. Cut or shred cabbage coarsely. Soak in cold water for at least 15 minutes.

Fry bacon pieces in deep pan. Remove cabbage from water and place in pan. Simmer for 10 minutes with bacon and grease, stirring occasionally. Add apples and caraway seeds.

Combine vinegar, sugar or honey, salt and wine then pour over cabbage. Cover and simmer for 1 hour and 15 minutes. If liquid remains after cooking, uncover and simmer until liquid is absorbed.
Makes 6 to 8 servings.

Walnut Garlic Sauce

A delicious sauce that turns plain steamed vegetables into a special dish.

2 egg yolks
2 tablespoons white wine vinegar
1 tablespoon lemon juice
3 garlic cloves
1/2 teaspoon salt
1 cup olive oil
1/2 cup ground walnuts

Place egg yolks, vinegar, lemon juice, garlic and salt in blender. Mix well. With blender on lowest speed, gradually add oil, blending until smooth. Stir in walnuts. Makes about 2 cups.

Sam Jasper Winery's grape crusher, 1948.

Back of the winery in 1948.

Zippy Zucchini Spears

6 long, slender zucchini
2 tablespoons each green and red peppers
2 tablespoons fresh parsley, finely chopped
2 green onions, finely chopped
1 clove garlic, crushed
1/2 cup olive oil
1/4 cup wine vinegar
2 teaspoons sugar
1/4 cup California dry white wine

Trim ends from zucchini, but do not peel. Cut into lengthwise strips, 4 strips to each half zucchini.

Steam for 2 to 3 minutes until al dente. Drain and place in shallow dish. Combine remaining ingredients and pour over zucchini. Marinate 2 hours. Serve a cold vegetable with marinade or drain, using zucchini spears as garnish.
Serves 4

Fourth Generation Cousins in 2008:
Danton, Brad, Dominick, Camdan, and Caterina

Fruits

Cantaloupe In Viognier

Take along on a picnic—add nuts at the last minute.

1 cantaloupe (or a combination of melons except watermelon)
California Viognier wine
Crushed pistachios

Cut melon in half and remove the liquid, seeds and shreds. Scoop out flesh in bite-size pieces and place in glass bowl. Pour wine over melon to cover. Chill. Serve fruit in dessert dishes with some wine. Sprinkle crushed pistachios on top at the last minute to maintain crunch.

SKI LODGE REWARD
(Mulled red wine)

1 orange
6 to 8 whole cloves
3 cinnamon sticks
2 bottles California Zinfandel (750 ml)
1/2 cup sugar

Stud orange with cloves. Set aside.
Mix wine with sugar in crock pot. Add orange and cinnamon sticks. Simmer covered until hot. Serve directly from crock pot into 8 ounce mugs.
Serves 6

Poached Zinfandel Figs

Zinfandel is wonderful to use for poaching fruit. Try plums for a seasonal change.

1-1/2 cups California Zinfandel wine
3 tablespoons honey
2 pounds fresh purple figs, stems removed
Whipping cream
Vanilla (optional)

Bring wine and honey to a boil. Add figs. Reduce heat and simmer fruit for 20 minutes. Cool figs in liquid and chill. Serves 6 to 8.
    Serve with plain, thick cream or whip with a dash of vanilla.

Original Sam-Jasper Winery, in 1948.

Zabaglione

Although traditionally prepared with Marsala wine, this frothy custard gives zabaglione a new twist.

6 eggs, separated
1/3 cup sugar
1/2 cup California Viognier wine
Zest from one lemon
24 fresh blackberries

Beat egg yolks in top of double boiler over hot water. Gradually add sugar and wine. Whisk continually until mixture thickens, increases in volume and is heated thoroughly. This may take as long as 10 minutes. Do not let mixture boil. Remove from heat. Reserve 1/2 cup of custard in separate container.

Beat egg whites until stiff and fold into thickened custard. Spoon into 6 to 8 martini glasses and arrange blackberries on top. Drizzle reserved custard over berries and sprinkle generously with lemon zest. This fragile dessert does not chill or keep. Serve immediately.

Variations: Omitting egg whites, you may use this custard as a sauce to spoon over your favorite fresh fruit or present as a pudding, served in small portions.

Baked Apple Slices

This lightly sweet dish doubles as a side dish for roast pork, turkey or ham.

6 tart apples
Butter, as needed
3/4 cup California Zinfandel wine
3/4 cup brown sugar
2 cinnamon sticks
Zest from ground 1/2 lemon
Nutmeg for garnish

Peel and core apples, trimming off tops and bottoms. Slice into 1/4-inch thick rings. Sauté gently in butter for 5 minutes. Arrange in baking dish and pour wine over them. Sprinkle with sugar. Place cinnamon sticks in wine then add lemon zest and nutmeg. Bake at 325° until apples are soft (about 45 minutes). Serve hot as a dessert, with whipped cream or ice cream. Also delicious cold as a side dish. Serves 6.

Wine Suggestion: California red dessert wine

MAKE YOUR OWN ICE BLOCK

Create your own ice block to fit the occasion and the size of your bowl.

Punches may be diluted slightly without changing their basic flavor and balance of liquids but should be watched carefully. When the ice block has melted considerably and your party is still in full swing, replace the melted block with a fresh piece of ice.

Striped Effect Ice Block

Take a half-gallon milk carton or ice cream carton and fill one-fourth full of water. Freeze. On top of ice, lay thinly sliced orange slices, cucumber slices, lemon rounds or other fruits or vegetables, overlapping slightly. Fill to one-half full. Freeze. Repeat procedure until you have a full block with three colorful layers.

Colored Ice Block

Create a striped effect by using colored water or fruit juices. Follow the procedure above.

Individual Ice Cubes

When serving punch from a pitcher, you may wish to place an individual ice cube into each cup or glass. For a decorative effect, put a long-stemmed cherry, a quarter-slice of lemon, or a pineapple piece into each ice cube tray before filling with water.

Baked Pears With Ginger

A simple preparation for an elegant dessert.

8 to 10 small, firm pears (Bosc pears work well)
1/2 cup sugar
1/2 teaspoon lemon rind
2 cups California Zinfandel wine

Peel pears, leaving stems on. Preheat oven to 350°. Mix sugar, lemon rind and wine in shallow baking dish. Place pears upright in dish and bake about an hour or until tender. Baste pears frequently.

Combine Ginger Cream ingredients and serve with warm or chilled pears. Serves 8.

GINGER CREAM:

1/2 pint heavy cream, whipped
1/4 cup powdered sugar
1 tablespoon finely grated fresh ginger

PEACH WITH ZINFANDEL
(Pesca Con Vino Rosso)

Fruit-flavored wine has been an Italian favorite for a long time. The wine is sipped with the meal and the fruit eaten as a dessert. Apple, orange, plum and peach slices take this favorite through the seasons.

1 large peach, peeled and sliced
2 ounces chilled California Zinfandel wine

Place peeled peach slices in a pitcher. Add a dry red wine, preferably a fruity Zinfandel. Let sit for an hour.

Or make a single serving by placing several peach slices in a glass, then filling with wine.

Fruit Compote

Ripe, fresh fruit gives the best results. Wonderful with hot, mulled red wine. (pg.126)

1-1/2 cups crumbled coconut macaroon cookies
1-1/2 cups fresh plums, sliced
3 cups peaches, sliced and peeled
1-1/2 cups strawberries, halved
1/4 cup firmly packed brown sugar
1/2 cup California cream sherry wine

Lightly butter a baking dish. Cover bottom with layer of macaroon crumbs. Add a layer each of plums, peaches and berries. Alternate crumb and fruit layers, ending with crumbs. Sprinkle brown sugar and sherry on top.

Bake 20 to 30 minutes at 350° or until fruit is fork-tender. Serve warm. Serves 8

Crystallized Grapes

Serve several clusters in sherbet glasses as dessert or use as a garnish for meat platters and fruit salads.

1 large cluster seedless green grapes (about 1 pound)
2 egg whites
1 tablespoon California Moscato wine
Finely granulated sugar

Divide cluster into bunches of approximately 8 to 10 grapes. Combine egg whites and wine, beating until blended but not foamy. Dip grapes into egg/wine mixture then sprinkle with sugar. Place in single layer on attractive serving platter. Place in refrigerator until glazed and hardened. Serve cold.

Note: A combination of purple, red and green grapes is attractive interspersed with thin slices of summer melons. Serve with California sparkling wine or Chardonnay.

Joe Sciabica, Jr., grandson of Gaspare, dipping apples into wine glass. Joe retired as a member of the Senior Executive Service for the Department of the Air Force in 2015 after 33 years of service to our nation.

Peach Topping

Delicious over ice cream.

2 large peaches, peeled and sliced (about two cups)
1/4 cup sugar
1/2 cup California Viognier wine
3 whole allspice berries
Freshly grated nutmeg to taste

To peel whole peach, place in boiling water for 10 to 20 seconds. Remove loosened skin and peach stone. Slice peach into 4-inch slices. Heat sugar and wine in saucepan over medium heat until sugar dissolves. Add allspice and nutmeg. Stir and pour over peaches. Cover and refrigerate, stirring occasionally, until well chilled. Serve over vanilla, cinnamon or butterscotch ice cream.
Serves 4.

Variation: Combine peaches with other fruits for a fresh salad.

Vince and General Thomas P. Stafford, USAF (RET) enjoying a cold one at Joe's retirement party.

Note: General Stafford was commander of Apollo in May1969, first flight of the lunar module to the moon. General Stafford was cited in the Guinness Book of World Records for the highest speed ever attained by man. During Apollo 10 reentry, the spacecraft attained 24,791 statute miles per hour.

FRESH FRUIT SALAD

Last-minute assembly of ingredients makes a truly fresh fruit salad. White wine or citrus juice keeps the fruit from discoloring.

Strawberries—Store unwashed and uncovered in refrigerator. Hull and wash strawberries just before adding to salad.

Raspberries—To wash, place in colander and let water flow gently through them. Drain and shake lightly. Use berries at once.

Peaches—Peel fresh peaches by dropping in hot water for 10 seconds. Dip next in cold water and peel skin off in strips.

Melons—Refrigerate melons only long enough to chill or delicate flavors will be lost. To form melon balls, cut melon in half horizontally, remove seeds and scoop out flesh with a small ball scoop.

Pears—Pears discolor and soften quickly so add to salad at the last minute.

Bananas—Slightly firm bananas are best in salads. Slice them just before serving to prevent discoloration.

Kiwi Fruit—Cut in half lengthwise and scoop out flesh with a spoon or peel and slice thinly.

Apricots—Pit apricots by cutting in half with a knife, following the seam. Twist the two halves in opposite directions to separate them and remove the pit.

Fruit Dressings

I.

1/2 cup California dry sherry wine
1/4 cup honey
Juice of 1 lemon
Dash salt

Blend ingredients thoroughly and pour over your favorite tart fruits—apples, grapefruits, oranges, etc.

II.

This simple dressing is good over hulled and sliced strawberries or served as a dip alongside unhulled strawberries.

1/2 cup sour cream
2 tablespoons California Moscato wine
1 tablespoon honey

III.

This creamy dressing is delicious on fruit salad. Try a combination of diced fresh pineapple, oranges and apples. Add tiny marshmallows for an old-fashioned taste.

1 package cream cheese (3 ounces)
1 tablespoon lemon juice
1 tablespoon sugar
1/4 cup California dry sherry wine
Dash salt

Soften cream cheese. Gradually add lemon juice and remaining ingredients, blending well.

Sweets

Spanish Basque Flan

Former Delicato employee Joe Larranaga shared this recipe. "It tastes just like a dish from my family's native country," Joe said.

3/4 cup sugar
6 eggs, well beaten
3/4 cup sugar
1 quart milk
1-1/2 teaspoons vanilla
1 tablespoon brandy (optional)
1/4 teaspoon salt
3 cinnamon sticks

Place 3/4 cup sugar in pan over medium heat. Shake pan until sugar begins to melt. Stir continually as syrup bubbles and turns from golden brown to rich brown. When syrup begins to caramelize on bottom of pan, check for thickness. Draw a "path" across bottom of pan with a wooden spoon. Consistency is right when syrup seeps slowly back, covering path. Remove immediately from heat and pour into heatproof bowl. Turn bowl around quickly so caramel coats sides evenly. (It looks like a lacquer coating inside the bowl.) Set aside.

Beat eggs until thick and lemon-colored. Blend in sugar, then whisk milk into sugar mixture. Add vanilla, brandy and salt. Strain into caramelized bowl. Place cinnamon sticks on top like hands of clock. Put bowl in shallow pan of hot water (9 x 13-inch cake pan works well). Bake in 325° oven for about one hour or until knife inserted in center of flan comes out clean.

Chill overnight or at least 8 hours in refrigerator before inverting on plate to serve. Spoon caramelized syrup over each serving.
Serves 10.

Enjoy a cup of coffee and a glass of California cream sherry with this rich, creamy dessert.

SHERRIED COFFEE

Chilled or steaming, this drink finishes a good meal and a delightful evening.

8 cups strong, black coffee
1 cup light corn syrup
1 quart ice water
2 cups cream sherry wine
1 cup heavy cream, whipped

Combine coffee and corn syrup in saucepan, stirring continually. Bring to a boil, pour coffee into a bowl. Blend in ice water and sherry.

Ladle from bowl or pour from a pitcher. Top with a dollop of whipped cream. Serves 12 to 14.

Variation: If hot coffee is preferred, use boiling water and heated sherry. Serve immediately.

4th generation cousins celebrating Mollie's birthday in 1999.
Left to Right: Jeanette, Katie, Mollie, Stephen, Kyle.

Belinda's Torte

A four-layer cake with a surprising snap of chocolate and a crunch of almonds. It was Belinda Cardoza's contribution to this year's family sausage making potluck supper.

1 box chocolate cake mix (2 layer size)
8 ounces sweet chocolate
3/4 cup butter, room temperature
1/2 cup toasted almonds, coarsely chopped
2 cups whipped cream (or 8 ounces Cool Whip)

Bake cake in 2 lightly greased and floured 9-inch layer pans. Cool. Split each layer horizontally.

Melt 6 ounces of chocolate in double boiler over hot water. Cool slightly and beat in butter. Add almonds.

Spread one cake layer with half of chocolate mixture. Top with second layer and spread it with half of the whipped cream. Spread remaining chocolate on third layer and finish with whipped cream on top of the last layer.

Decorate with chocolate shavings made from remaining 2 ounces of chocolate. Refrigerate until ready to serve.

Serves 12 to 16.

Hint: For easier slicing, dip long-blade knife into glass of warm water before each cut. Wipe knife blade clean after slicing and dip in water again.

At home, dessert was mainly homemade cakes or cookies. When we felt like something sweet we whipped up what we called the one egg cake. We beat the batter by hand, for we never had an electric mixer, spiced it up with Raleigh's vanilla, baked it, and ate it without frosting.

— Frances Sciabica

Four Generations: Mary, Dorothy, Marie, Jeanette in 2005.

Still making doughnuts in 2010.

Mom called these doughnuts 'malasadas',
Dad called these doughnuts 'filozes'.
No one won the argument, that I can
remember.

— Dorothy Indelicato

Dorothy as middle queen in
Portuguese festa parade, 1940.

Portuguese Doughnuts

Filozes is pronounced: fee lōj. This version is made with baking powder, so it's quick!

2 cups milk
5 eggs
1/2 cup granulated sugar
1 teaspoon salt
4 cups all-purpose flour
4 teaspoon baking powder
Vegetable oil for deep-frying

Heat oil to 375°F.

In large bowl, whisk eggs until foamy. Beat in ½ cup sugar and salt until well blended. In separate bowl, blend flour and baking powder. Gradually beat flour into egg batter alternately with milk until smooth.

Each filozes is roughly 2 tablespoons of batter. Once the batter balls are in the oil, lower heat immediately to medium-low (adjust heat to keep doughnuts from browning too quickly).
    Cook for about 10 minutes, turning once, until golden-brown all over. Drain on paper towels.
Makes 36 doughnuts

Coating:
1 cup granulated sugar
1 teaspoon ground cinnamon

    Place sugar and ground cinnamon in a small paper bag. Put paper bag in a quart-sized plastic bag so that the coating stays contained. Place 2 or 3 doughnuts at a time in the paper bag and shake to cover doughnuts evenly. Set on paper towels.

Portuguese Doughnuts, Original Recipe

Filozes are deeper in color than American doughnuts. The irregular shapes resemble brown leaves with upturned edges.

1-1/2 cups milk, lukewarm (105°-1150)
1/2 cup warm water
1/2 cup sugar
2 teaspoons salt
2 packages dry yeast (1/4 ounce each)
2 eggs, room temperature, slightly beaten
1/2 cup soft butter
7 to 7-1/2 cups sifted flour
1/4 cup milk
Vegetable oil for frying
Granulated sugar

Three generations, making Portuguese doughnuts. Dorothy Indelicato, Mary Cardoza and Marie Indelicato, 1985.

Add yeast to warm water, stirring until completely dissolved. Set aside.

Mix milk, sugar and salt and combine with yeast mixture. Add eggs and butter. Add flour in 2 additions, kneading mixture until dough is easy to handle and does not stick to hands. Place in lightly greased bowl and turn once so entire dough ball is greased. Let rise until it doubles in size. Punch down and let it rise a second time.

Dip fingers in small bowl of milk, then pinch off about 2 tablespoons of dough. Holding dough in both hands, use fingertips and thumbs to stretch dough into a 4-inch circle. Avoid thick edges by stretching until circle is thin throughout. Don't worry about small tears. Holding dough in hands, poke hole in center of circle from underneath with a finger before carefully placing into 2 inches of hot oil. Brown doughnuts on each side, about 2 minutes. Remove to drain on paper towels.

Coating:

Place sugar and ground cinnamon in a small paper bag. Put paper bag in a quart-sized plastic bag so that the coating stays contained. Place 2 or 3 doughnuts at a time in the paper bag and shake to cover doughnuts evenly. Set on paper towel. Eat the same day or freeze after baking. Makes 4 dozen.

Variation: Some prefer a thin layer of light corn syrup drizzled on the doughnuts.

Kolácky

4 cups flour
1/2 teaspoon salt
1 cake yeast (1 ounce)
3/4 pound butter
6 egg yolks
1/2 pint sour cream
Powdered sugar for dusting

Sift flour with salt into large bowl. Crumble in yeast, mixing well. Gradually add small amounts of butter, cutting into flour by criss crossing mixture with two table knives until butter is incorporated into flour. Add egg yolks and sour cream, mixing until smooth.

Gather dough into a ball, turning until all flour is removed from bottom of bowl. Place in refrigerator overnight.

Lightly flour and sugar surface for rolling dough. Cut dough ball into 4 pieces. Roll each piece into 4-inch squares, 1/4 inch thick. (Allow proportionately more filling per pastry and a few additional minutes baking time for larger cookies.) Roll each square again for additional thinness.

Place 1 teaspoon walnut filling on one corner of square. Roll up lightly to opposite corner. Place pastry seam-side down on ungreased baking sheet, 1/2 inch apart. Bake at 325° for 20 to 25 minutes, until lightly brown. Let cool and remove to plate. Sift powdered sugar lightly on top.

WALNUT FILLING:

3 cups ground walnuts
1-1/2 cups sugar
1 tablespoon lemon juice
4 tablespoons lukewarm water

Combine walnuts and sugar. Stir in lemon juice and enough water to make mixture moist but firm (about 4 tablespoons).
Recipe makes approximately 8 dozen cookies.

SICILIAN GRANITA

1 bottle of California Merlot (750 ml)
2 cups water
3/4 cup sugar
2 tablespoons grated lemon peel
1 cinnamon stick
2 tablespoons lemon juice

Combine wine, water, sugar, lemon peel and cinnamon stick in saucepan. Bring to a boil, stirring often, until sugar dissolves. Reduce heat and simmer five minutes, uncovered.

Cool mixture to room temperature. Add lemon juice and remove cinnamon stick. Pour mixture in shallow pans (9 x 13-inch cake pans work well) and freeze overnight.

Using a fork, scratch top of mixture to loosen and spoon into individual bowls. Garnish with fresh fruits such as orange, melon, pear or peach slices or serve simply with mint garnish.
Serves 8 to 10.

Hats off to family rides!

Tapioca Pudding

2/3 cup sugar
6 tablespoons tapioca
5 1/2 cups milk
2 eggs well beaten
2 teaspoons vanilla
Ground cinnamon (optional)

Mix sugar, tapioca, milk, eggs in a large microwavable bowl.
Let stand for five minuttes.

Microwave for a total of 12 minutes until mixture comes to a boil. Be sure to stir after every three minutes.

Remove from microwave and add vanilla.
Serve warm or chilled; Sprinkle cinnamon for garnish.
Serves 8.

My son-in-law, Kim Mathews, designed the landscaping around the tasting room.

Chocolate Mousse

6 ounces semisweet chocolate
5 eggs, separated
1 teaspoon vanilla
2 teaspoons brewed coffee
1 cup heavy cream
3 tablespoons California Moscato wine
1/4 cup sugar
Chocolate shavings

Melt chocolate in double boiler. Beat egg yolks to lemon color and gradually stir into chocolate. Add vanilla and coffee. Remove from heat.

In mixing bowl, beat cream until thick. Stir in wine and fold mixture into chocolate. In another bowl, beat egg whites and sugar until stiff. Carefully fold into chocolate mixture. Pour into individual dessert dishes. Top with chocolate shavings. Chill for at least 2 hours. Cover tightly with plastic wrap so crust will not form on top of mousse. Serves 6 to 8.

TOP HAT

3/4 cup California Pinot Noir wine
1/3 cup orange juice
1 tablespoon powdered sugar
Ice cubes
1 tablespoon California port wine
Fresh fruit to garnish

Stir Pinot Noir, orange juice and sugar in a tall glass until sugar dissolves. Add ice cubes. Float port on top. Garnish with fruit. Makes a single serving.

Mary Celsi Indelicato

Anise Cookies

This is a favorite Indelicato family recipe.

1 cup sugar
1/2 cup butter (1 cube)
1 tablespoon anise seeds, crushed
3 eggs
3 cups flour
3 teaspoons baking powder
1/2 teaspoon salt
Milk
Sesame seeds (optional)

Mix sugar with butter and anise seeds. Beat in eggs. Sift flour, baking powder, and salt together and add to mixture.

On lightly floured surface shape dough with hands into loaves 2-inches wide x 1/2 inch thick on cookie sheet. Lightly flatten with fingers. Brush with milk and sprinkle with sesame seeds, if desired. Bake at 350° for 20 minutes or until golden.

Remove from oven. Immediately cut into 1/2 to 3/4-inch diagonal slices. Return to oven and bake for an additional 15 minutes until lightly toasted. Makes about 48 cookies.

Cranberry Apple Pie

2 pie crusts (9-inch)
5 cups Granny Smith apples, peeled and sliced
1-1/2 cups fresh, uncooked cranberries
1 cup sugar
3 tablespoons flour
1/2 teaspoon cinnamon
Dash salt
1 teaspoon butter
1 teaspoon sugar and 1/4 teaspoon cinnamon, mixed
Whipped cream (optional)
2 tablespoons California Moscato wine

Preheat oven to 400°. Place bottom crust in pie plate and refrigerate while making the filling.

Combine apples, cranberries, sugar, flour, cinnamon and salt. Toss lightly. Spoon mixture into chilled pie crust. Add dabs of butter. Roll out second crust. Place over fruit, slitting top for vents. Sprinkle with mixture of cinnamon and sugar.

Bake 40 minutes at 400°. Serve pie at room temperature with whipped cream or with thin slices of mild cheddar cheese.
Serves 8.

JANE'S APPLE CAKE

3 eggs
1 cup oil
2 cups sugar
1 teaspoon vanilla
2 cups flour
1 teaspoon baking soda
½ teaspoon salt
2 teaspoons cinnamon
4 cups peeled, cored and sliced tart apples
1 cup large walnut pieces

Coat a 9" x 13" baking pan with non-stick spray.

Pre-hat oven to 350°.

Beat eggs & oil together until frothy. Add sugar & vanilla, mixing thoroughly. Sift together and add flour, baking soda, salt & cinnamon, mixing thoroughly. Add apples & nuts and mix until evenly distributed in the batter. Pour into prepared pan and bake 45 minutes or until very brown.

Pumpkin Squares

4 eggs
2 cups sugar
1 cup salad oil
1 can pumpkin (29 ounces)
3-1/2 cups sifted flour
3 teaspoons cinnamon
1-1/4 teaspoons salt
2 teaspoons baking soda
2 tablespoons California medium sherry wine
1-1/2 cups chopped walnuts
3/4 cup raisins

Mix sugar and eggs. Add oil and pumpkin. Sift flour with cinnamon, salt and baking soda. Add to pumpkin mixture. Stir in sherry. Add nuts and raisins.

Pour into lightly greased 14 x 20-inch pan. Bake 35 to 40 minutes at 350°. This dessert keeps well refrigerated for several days or can be frozen. Serve plain or with whipped cream.
Makes 24 squares.

Apricot Upside-Down Cake

It is fun to make this cake fresh in the morning to bring to the office while it is still warm. The cousins each try to get to the cake first to claim a corner - their favorite part. It is not unusual to have all four corners missing from the cake before the rest of the office staff gets to the break room.

This good natured competition over who gets the corners is reminiscent of my own sibling rivalries.

-- Dorothy Indelicato

2/3 cube of butter
1 pound dark brown sugar, less 1/2 cup
24 apricot halves from 2 cans (17oz. each)
3/4 cup walnuts, chopped coarsly
1 box white or yellow cake mix

Melt butter in a 9" x 13" glass baking dish. Sprinkle the dark brown sugar over the melted butter. Mash well with a fork until all of the butter and brown sugar are mixed and appear "crumbly". Arrange 24 apricot halves with the cut sides down evenly in rows in the baking dish. Place the walnut pieces around the apricot halves to fill in spaces.

Prepare cake mix per box instructions. After the cake batter is prepared, pour the batter over the apricots/walnut/brown sugar topping.

Bake per cake mix instructions, usually 350° for 35 - 40 minutes until a wooden toothpick comes out clean and dry when placed in the middle of the cake.

Remove cake from the oven and allow to cool 5 minutes. Release cake from the dish by running a knife around the perimeter, between the cake and the 9" x 13" baking dish. Place a heatproof serving platter over the top of cake and turn the baking dish upside down on to the platter.
Serve warm or cold.
Makes 24 squares.

Hint: Should any apricots remain on the baking dish, simply use a fork to place the offending apricot(s) back on the cake.
Makes 24 squares.

Postscript

Now, more than ninety years after Dad planted the first vines in 1924, there are three wineries producing award-winning wines from several thousand acres of family vineyards with distribution to more than 35 countries around the world.

Through all of these changes and growth, we have never lost sight of the fact that this is more than just a livelihood. It is the realization of the dream of our father, grandfather, and great-grandfather. The young Italian immigrant, who came to this country seeking a better life, would be extremely proud to see what has been accomplished by his family.

We are blessed to be able to continue his dream of the good life in the United States.
---- Vincent Indelicato

Back row, 3rd generation: Cheryl, Frank, Jr., Marie, Chris, Jay, Mike
Front row, 2nd generation: Frank Sr., Vince, Dorothy

INDEX

APPETIZERS:
Antipasto Tray 29
Artichoke Bites 29
Biscotti 28
Caponata 30
Carpaccio 34
Chicken Wings 32
Cozzola 33
Garlic Galore 28
Lemon Shrimp 30
Little Pizzas 31
Sherried Walnuts 32
Spinach Squares 31

SOUPS:
Apple-Lemon Soup 44
Beef-Cheddar Chowder 38
California Onion Soup 42
Caterina's Minestrone 36
Chilled Apricot Soup 38
Consommé with Avocado 37
Kale Soup 40
Mushroom Soup 39
Oyster Chowder 37
Pea Soup 41
Pear & Celery Soup 44
Spinach Soup 43
Spoon Bread 43

SALADS:
Basic Vinaigrette 53
Chick Pea Salad 52
Chicken Marinade (Salad) 48
French Potato Salad 51
Glistening Rice 48
Little Caesar Salad 46
Minted Tomato Salad 50
Oriental Chicken Salad 48
Pea Pods 48
Salad Dressing 49
Scallop Salad 49
Tossed Spinach Salad 47
Vineyard Vinaigrette 54
Watercress 48
White Wine Salad Dressing 54

PASTA:
Anchovy Sauce 57
Ascuitta 58
Caterina's Pasta Ascuitta 58
Crunchy Brown Rice 79
Garlic Pasta Sauce 62
Mushroom Sauce 59
Pasta Tips 56
Pasta Topping 59
Pesto for Pasta 61

Rabbit (with Pasta) 58
Pesto For Pasta 61
Shells and Zucchini 62
Spaghetti Ragu 60
Today's Tomato Sauce 57
Vermaicelli with Mint 60
Winter Vegetable Sauce 61
Zucchini and Shells 62

SEAFOOD:
Baked Perch 66
Basic Marinade 26
Cod Navarro Style 72
Delta Catfish with Garlic 65
Dorothy's Cioppino 71
Grilled Whole Trout 67
Homer's Marinaded Crab 69
Joe's Garlic Sauce 72
Lemon Shrimp 30
Lumache (Snails) 71
Mustard Sauce for Fish 70
Paprika Sauce 70
Scallop Sauté 68
Spirited Sole 67
Sumptuous Snapper 66
Sweet and Sour Sauce 70

POULTRY:
Basic Marinade 25, 26, 48
Chardonnay Chicken 74
Chicken Cacciatori 74
Chicken in Feta Sauce 80
Chicken in Moscato 78
Chicken in Zinfandel 82
Chicken on the Hot Side 85
Chicken Wings 32
Chicken with Nutmeg 79
Chicken with Okra 81
Chicken with Spices 84
Classic Chicken in Wine 75
Coq Au Vin 76
Italian Stuffed Turkey 86
Mustard Chicken 76
North Italian Stuffed 87
Persian Chicken 83
Port Marinade 82
Rabbit Stew 88
Roast Chicken 77
Rowdy Chicken 77
Sesame Sauce 78
South Italian Stuffed Turkey 87

BEEF & LAMB:
Basic Beef Burgundy 90
Basic Marinade 24, 26
Beef with Mushroom Soup 91
Round Steak & Mushrooms 94
Beef with Blue Cheese 93
Braised Beef Short Ribs 104
Carpaccio 34
Chorizo Meatballs 95
Dot's Beef Stew 92
Francy's Beef Stew 92
Gremolata 103
Lamb Chops 98
Lamb with Orange 100
Leg of Lamb 100
Mary's Pot Roast 93
Osso Buco 103
Ox Tail Stew 101
Peppery Kebabs 96
Polenta 104
Portuguese Sopas 97
Rabbit Stew 88
Shish Kebabs (Lamb) 99
Steak Joan 96
Veal with Brandy Cream 102
Veal with Champagne 102

PORK:
Chops with Wild Rice 114
Cranberry Apples 110
Family Sausages 108, 109
Ham Baked in Wine 110
Pork and Sage Supper 112
Pork Chops with Fennel 111
Sweet and Sour Pork 113

VEGETABLES:
Ana's Portuguese Fava Beans 117
Broccoli in White Wine 116
California Onion Soup 42
Corn Baked in Foil 99
Curried Walnut 121
Herbed Cabbage 119
Onions in Wine 110
Pea Pods 48
Portuguese Beans 118
Red Cabbage 122
Red Pepper Gratin 120
Sherried Asparagus 119
Sherried Sweet Potatoes 121
Spinach Soup 43
Squash Cups 121
Sweet and Sour Onions 117
Vegetable Kebabs 122
Walnut Garlic Sauce 123
Watercress Salad 48
Zippy Zucchini Spears 124
Zucchini Bread 41

FRUITS:
Apple Cake, Jane's 139
Baked Apple Slices 127
Baked Pears with Ginger 128
Cantaloupe in Viognier 126
Cranberry Mold 87
Crystallized Grapes 129
Fruit Compote 128
Fruit Salad Dressings 130
Peach Topping 129
Peach with Zinfandel 128
Poached Zinfandel Figs 126

SWEETS:
Anise Cookies 138
Apricot Upside-Down Cake 140
Belinda's Torte 133
Biscotti 28
Cheese Blintzes 137
Chocolate Mousse 138
Cranberry Apple Pie 139
Granita Sicilian Ice 136
Jane's Apple Cake 139
Kolacky 136
Popovers 41
Portuguese Doughnuts 134, 135
Pumpkin Squares 139
Roasted Walnuts 129
Sherried Walnuts 32
Spanish Basque Flan 132
Tapioca Pudding 137
Zabaglione 127
Zucchini Bread 41

WINE DRINKS:
After Ski Reward 126
Chardonnay Mint Julips 113
Ice Blocks 127
Peach with Zinfandel 128
Pinot Noir Valencia 93
Royal Red- 44
Sherried Coffee 132
Ski Lodge Reward 126
Strawberry Sangria 26
Summertime Sangria 23
Ten Second Sangria 138
Top Hat 138

MISCELLANEOUS:
Crunchy Brown Rice 79
Curried Walnuts 121
Glistening Rice 48
Grape Jelly 98
Mesquite 24
Polenta 104
Red Wine Mustard 109
Spoon Bread 43
Wild Rice 114
Wine Jelly 98

FROM THE "COOKING WITH WINE" SERIES

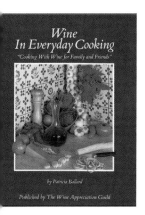

WINE IN EVERYDAY COOKING
Patricia Ballard
Paperback, 81/2x11", 128pp
$9.95
ISBN: 978-0-932664-45-7

**CALIFORNIA WINE LOVERS'
COOKBOOK**
Malcolm Hebert
Paperback, 81/2x11", 176pp
$12.95
ISBN: 978-0-932664-82-2

**GOURMET WINE COOKING THE
EASY WAY**
wine Advisory Board
Paperback, 81/2x11",128pp
$12.95
ISBN: 978-0-932664-01-3

FINE WINE IN FOOD
Patricia Ballard
Paperback, 81/2x11",144pp
$12.95
ISBN: 978-0-932664-56-3

**EPICUREAN RECIPES OF
CALIFORNIA WINEMAKERS**
Wine Advisory Board
Paperback, 81/2x11",128pp
$12.95
ISBN: 978-0-932664-00-6

**FAVORITE RECIPES OF
CALIFORNIA WINEMAKERS**
Wine Advisory Board
Paperback, 81/2x11",128pp
$12.95
ISBN: 978-0-932664-03-7

FROM THE "ITALIAN PANTRY" SERIES

PASTA
Fabrizio Ungaro
Hardcover, 8x9", 64pp
$12.95
ISBN: 978-1-891267-56-7

PROSCIOTTO
Carla Bardi
Hardcover, 8x9", 64pp
$12.95
ISBN: 978-1-891267-56-7

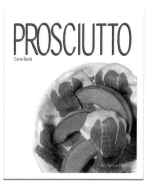

ozes

ozes are deeper in color than American doughnuts. The irregular
apes resemble brown leaves with upturned edges.

1/2 cups milk, lukewarm (105°-115°)
2 cup warm water (105°-115°)
2 cup sugar
easpoons salt
packages dry yeast (1/4 ounce each)
eggs, room temperature, slightly beaten
2 cup soft margarine or shortening
to 7-1/2 cups sifted flour
/4 cup milk
il for frying
ranulated sugar or white corn syrup

dd yeast to warm water, stirring until completely dissolved. Set aside.
Mix milk, sugar and salt and combine with yeast mixture. Add eggs and
margarine or shortening. Add flour in 2 additions, kneading mixture
ntil dough is easy to handle and does not stick to hands. Place in lightly
reased bowl and turn once so entire dough ball is greased. Let rise until
ouble. Punch down and let rise a second time.

Dip fingers in small bowl of milk, then pinch off about 2
ablespoons of dough. Holding dough in both hands, use fingertips and
humbs to stretch dough into a 4-inch circle. Avoid thick edges by
stretching until circle is thin throughout. Don't worry about small tears.
Holding dough in hands, poke hole in center of circle from underneath
with middle finger. Keep hands wet with milk while forming
doughnuts.

Carefully place in 2 inches of hot shortening. Brown doughnuts on
one side, about 2 minutes. Using tongs, flip over to other side and fry
until brown. Remove to drain on absorbent paper. While hot, sprinkle
with granulated sugar or drizzle with corn syrup. Eat the same day or
freeze after baking. Makes 4 dozen.

If you double this recipe, you will use 5 lbs of flour, less 1 cup.

easpoon anchovy paste
/4 cup California dry sherry
tablespoon lemon juice
tablespoon minced parsley
/2 teaspoon dried mint
tablespoon butter
alt and pepper to taste

ook anchovy paste, sherry, lemon juice, parsley and mint in butter for 3
4 minutes. Taste for seasoning. Stir well and pour over hot fish.
Makes enough sauce for 1 large serving. Increase ingredients for
dditional servings.

II.

tablespoon butter
/4 cup chopped parsley
tablespoon minced fresh tarragon (or 1 teaspoon dried tarragon)
/2 cup California dry white wine

Melt butter. Stir in parsley, tarragon and wine. Cook over high heat for 1
minute, stirring constantly. Pour over hot fish. Makes a single serving.
Adjust amount of ingredients to number of servings.

135

each loaf makes approximate 32.

Soups

6 X recipe needs at least 19½ loa

6 X recipe made 563 oven spread in 11-17-07

(We ran out after 2

Making Port...
Three gene...
Indelicat...
Marie Indelicat...

In connection one 300° LOW 10 minutes

freeze before sending to soldier

Mom's Rice Pudding
1½ c rice
7 c milk
1 tsp vanilla
½ cube butter (¼ cup)
pinch salt

Washing jugs on Saturdays and Sundays to prepare for bottling the next day.